The 5th Conversation

You Didn't Close on the First Call. Here's How You Win Anyway

Tara Shuler | ConvoControl

Published by Carrot LLC
First Edition, 2026
ISBN: 979-8-9969530-7-3
Cover design by: Tara Shuler
Interior design by: Tara Shuler
For permissions, inquiries, or bulk orders, contact: questions@convocontrol.com
https://www.ConvoControl.com
"Everything is sales — because everything is a conversation".

Contents

Preface

Think about the last deal you lost. Did they actually tell you no, or did you just stop asking? Be honest. Nobody is watching. Your answer to that question is the reason this book exists.

Before I ever closed a deal, I learned how to fall. I was a Level 9 competitive gymnast, and later a gymnastics coach, and the sport handed me the one lesson I have used every day since: performance is trained, not hoped for. Nobody walks onto the floor and rises to the occasion. You fall back on how you have trained. Every single time.

Then I spent more than 25 years in sales. I closed over $50 million across B2B, B2C, and live events, and I did it in rooms where nobody handed me the deal. Along the way I learned what actually separates the people who close from the people who almost close. It is not talent. It is not the pitch. It is not even the first conversation.

It is what happens after the first conversation ends.

For two decades I watched the same scene play out on every sales floor I worked. A talented rep does the hard part. Finds the prospect. Gets the meeting. Runs a genuinely good first call. The prospect says it sounds interesting, they need to think about it, call me in a few weeks. And the rep sends one polite email, waits, and moves on to the next first call.

They did not lose that deal. They abandoned it.

Here is the part nobody says out loud: the one-call close is the exception, not the plan. Almost every deal that has ever closed took multiple conversations to get there. Yet almost all of our training goes into the first one. The opener. The pitch. The demo. Nobody trains the follow-up, so sellers improvise it, and improvisation under pressure is where deals go to die.

So I built the training. That is what this book is. Not a pile of tips, and not a stack of templates. A system for everything that happens after the first call: when to reach out, what to say, which channel to use, how to stay in control of a conversation that has gone quiet, and how to do all of it without ever becoming the pest you are afraid of being.

Every chapter ends with a drill, because knowing is not the same as owning. Most people read. Few people rep. If you run the reps on real deals in your real pipeline, this book will change what you close, not just what you know.

The deal goes to whoever is willing to have one more conversation. Let us train you to be that person.

Coach Tara

Introduction: The Deal You Already Paid For

You Did the Hard Part

Think about the last deal that didn't close on the first call. Not the one where the prospect flat-out said no. The one where they said it sounded interesting, they needed to think about it, they'd be in touch. And then they weren't.

And then you weren't either.

Who stopped first?

You prospected. You found a real person with a real problem and got them to agree to talk. That alone puts you ahead of most people who think about selling but never actually do it. You ran the conversation. You asked questions. You made the case. At the end of it, they didn't sign anything. So you moved on to the next one.

That's the moment this book is about. That pause between "let me think about it" and your next move. What you do in that pause decides whether you have a career or a grind.

Here's what most sellers do in that pause: nothing. Or one polite follow-up email. Then another week passes. Then reaching back out starts to feel awkward. Then the deal is gone. Not because the prospect chose someone else. Because nobody stayed in the conversation long enough to close it.

You did the hard part. And then you stopped right before the finish line.

Why the First Call Is Just the Opening Move

Most deals don't close on the first conversation. Research in sales performance, across industries and deal sizes, consistently finds that most closes happen after five or more touches. Not five pitches. Five conversations. Five moments where you show up, bring something worth hearing, and advance the dialogue.

Most sellers quit after one or two.

That gap is where this book lives. And that gap is costing you more than you've ever sat down to figure out.

The first conversation isn't the deal. It's the audition. You're showing the prospect you're worth talking to again. If you do it right, they want to hear from you. The problem is that most sellers treat silence after the first call as rejection, when it's almost always just life. The prospect got pulled into a back-to-back day. A vendor problem landed in their lap. Their weekend ran long. They didn't forget you. They got busy being busy.

Your job is to come back. With something specific. With value. With a question that's easier for them to answer than to ignore.

That's the whole system in two sentences. The chapters ahead show you how to run it, rep by rep.

The Three Real Enemies

Why don't sellers follow up? Ask most of them and they'll say they don't want to be a pest. Dig one layer deeper and you find three things doing the actual damage.

The first is fear. Specifically, the fear of being annoying. You don't call because some part of you believes that if they were interested, they would have called you. That belief is wrong, and Chapter 2 breaks down exactly why. Silence is almost never a verdict. It's a traffic jam.

The second is no system. You don't have a clear answer to "what do I do next?" so you do the default thing, which is nothing. You can't run a race without a course. Every day you sit down to follow up without a system is a day you're improvising under pressure, and improvising under pressure is where good intentions go to die.

The third is nothing to say. You burned through your pitch on the first call. The deck is already in their inbox. You can't send the same thing again and call it a follow-up. Saying "just checking in" feels desperate even as you type it, so you don't type it. You close the laptop and tell yourself you'll think of something better tomorrow.

You won't think of something better tomorrow. Tomorrow has its own first calls.

These three things, fear, no system, and nothing to say, are what this book is built to dismantle. Not with scripts or templates. With a trained approach to follow-up that puts you back in control of the conversation, even when the prospect has gone quiet.

How the Book Works

The book is organized in three parts.

Part One covers the head game. Chapters 1 through 5 deal with why you quit, what the numbers actually look like, how fear of being annoying is killing your pipeline, and how to see follow-up the way a trained professional sees it. You can't run the system if you're carrying mental weight that makes you stop before you've started.

Part Two is the system itself. Chapters 6 through 14 are the mechanics. When to reach out, how often, which channel to use, what to say, how to handle a ghost, and how to stay in deals that won't close for six more months. This is the section you'll flip back to when you're staring at a stalled pipeline and wondering what move comes next.

Part Three is the training. Chapters 15 through 17 are about making this a practice, not a project you attempt once and abandon. Consistency beats intensity every single time. One focused follow-up session a day builds more than five frantic hours on a Friday when you're desperate. These chapters turn the system into a habit.

Every chapter ends with a section called Your Rep. Three parts: The Drill, which is one action you take that day on a real deal in your real pipeline. The Questions, the exact questions you'll use to run the drill. And Train It, one line pointing you to where the reps continue after you close the book.

The Drill matters more than the chapter.

Most people read. Few people rep.

Reading and nodding along is comfortable. Pulling one deal out of your CRM and applying what you just read is where the skill actually builds. Every chapter asks you to do exactly that. The reps are small. Each one takes under an hour. But they compound. By the time you finish the book, you won't just know the system. You'll have practiced it on real deals, with real results showing up in your pipeline.

That's the difference between a book that changes how you think and a book that changes what you close.

The Fifth Conversation

From this page forward, "the fifth conversation" means something specific.

It means the conversation your competitors never got to.

It means the rep who stayed when everyone else quit. Who showed up again with something useful, with a real question, with the patience to understand that a "not yet" is still a conversation in progress. Who knew that silence after the first call is the starting line, not the finish.

Most sellers are gone by conversation two. A large share never follow up at all. The ones who reach conversation five are the ones closing deals nobody else even knew were still alive.

That pipeline is real. It exists right now, in your CRM or your notebook or your memory, full of conversations that started well and then got abandoned. Deals you paid for with your time, your energy, and your first call. Deals that are still warm enough to revive if you know what to say when you go back.

This book is the system for going back.

You already know how to open a conversation. This is the part nobody taught you: how to keep one going until it closes.

Chapter One

The Math of the Fifth Conversation

How many times do you follow up before you quit? Not the number you tell your manager. The real one.

For most sellers, the honest answer is uncomfortable. One touch. Maybe two. Then silence, because the silence feels safer than another message that might go unanswered. That instinct makes human sense. It is also the most expensive habit in sales.

There are two numbers that define a sales career. Not your close rate. Not your pipeline volume. These two numbers. Most sellers have never looked at both of them at the same time, which is exactly why the gap between them stays open year after year, filled with deals that could have closed and didn't.

The Two Numbers

The first number: most deals take five or more conversations before a buyer commits.

It holds across industries, deal sizes, and market conditions. High-ticket B2B, consumer services, coaching programs, live events. It doesn't matter much which market you're in. The pattern holds.

Think about why. Buyers have jobs. They have competing priorities. They have other people whose opinions matter to their decision. They have budget cycles, approval chains, and the very human tendency to wait until something feels urgent before committing. None of that changes in one call. A great first conversation plants the seed. It takes more conversations to grow it into a yes.

The one-call close happens. When it does, it feels like magic. But it is the outlier, not the standard. You can't build a system around the outlier.

The second number: most sellers follow up one or two times before they stop.

Some sellers never follow up at all after the first call. Most of the ones who do stop after one or two attempts, then shift their energy to the next new prospect, put more work into the top of the funnel, and wonder why their close rate stays flat.

Look at both numbers together. Five or more conversations to close. One or two touches before quitting.

That gap is where this book lives.

The Worked Example

Put real arithmetic on this, because the math makes the case better than any argument.

Picture a rep, call her Dana. She's good. She does her homework, asks decent questions, and runs a professional first conversation. Her quit number is two. She follows up once after the call, sometimes twice, and then moves on.

Dana has 100 first conversations a year. At one or two touches, she closes around ten percent of those conversations. That's ten deals from a hundred first calls. She thinks that's just her close rate. She's wrong. That's her quit-early close rate.

Now watch what happens when you extend the touches.

At touch three, four, and five, Dana isn't talking to the same people who went quiet earlier. She's reaching the ones who weren't ready yet. The person whose budget just opened. The one who finally got sign-off from a partner. The one who experienced the problem more acutely over the last six weeks and is now actively looking for exactly what Dana was describing in the first call.

Her close rate on those additional conversations is higher than her cold first-call rate, because the relationship already exists. The interest is established. The timing has improved. A deal that closes on touch five is a deal that was always closer to yes than it appeared after touch one.

Now add three more real touches to Dana's process. Meaningful touches, with questions and value, not just "just checking in" noise. Her close rate across the full sequence improves. She closes deals she would have walked away from. The pipeline she already built starts producing returns she wasn't capturing before.

Here's the part that changes how you think about this. The prospecting cost is identical either way. She found those hundred prospects regardless. She ran the first calls regardless. The only variable is whether she shows up again or disappears. Showing up costs almost nothing. The deals that come from it are not nothing.

That is the math of the fifth conversation.

The Graveyard Audit

Every seller has a graveyard. Most sellers have never looked at it honestly.

Open your CRM, your spreadsheet, your notebook, whatever you actually use. Go back twelve months. Find every deal that got one or two conversations and then went quiet on your side.

Now ask yourself one question for each one. Did that prospect tell you no?

Not "let me think about it." Not "call me next quarter." Not silence. A clear, explicit no.

For most sellers doing this audit honestly, the number of real rejections is much smaller than the number of abandoned deals. The prospect didn't say no. You just stopped asking.

That distinction changes everything.

When a prospect says no, the deal is over. You move on clean. When you abandon a deal before you've heard no, the deal is in limbo. The prospect hasn't rejected anything. They're waiting for someone to show up again. And if you don't show up, someone else will. In month three, when the budget opens. In month six, when the pain gets worse. In month eleven, when the season shifts and the decision finally becomes urgent.

Your graveyard is not a record of rejection. It is a record of deals you left for someone else to claim.

Picture a rep, call him Marcus. He does this audit and finds thirty-nine deals from the past year that received exactly one outreach after the first call. He can't tell you what happened to most of them, because he stopped tracking them the moment he stopped reaching out. He didn't lose those deals. He walked away from them before the conversation had a real chance to finish.

Do the audit. Count the deals. Count the actual touches. You'll find your real quit number, and it will show you something important about where your pipeline is bleeding out without you noticing.

The graveyard audit is uncomfortable. Do it anyway. The discomfort is useful information.

Follow-Up as the Highest-Paid Hour

Where does your highest-return sales activity actually live?

Most sellers say prospecting, because that's where they put most of their time. Cold outreach, cold calls, cold emails, networking, referral asks. All of it aimed at finding the next new person to talk to. That work matters. You need the top of the funnel. But look at the cost structure honestly.

Cold prospecting has a low conversion rate. It takes a significant amount of time per new conversation generated. Every relationship starts from zero. You have no rapport, no established interest, no shared history. You're convincing a stranger to give you their attention before you've earned any of it.

Now compare that to follow-up on a warm deal.

That prospect already took your call. They heard your value proposition. They gave you their time. Something you said got their attention enough to have a real conversation. The relationship started. The interest exists, even if the timing was off. The next touch costs you maybe five minutes. The upside is the full value of the deal. No new prospecting, no cold approach, no relationship to build from scratch.

That math is hard to beat.

Trained sellers protect follow-up time the way a competitive athlete protects conditioning. It's not glamorous. It doesn't generate the adrenaline of landing a new meeting. But it compounds in a way that cold work can't, because you're harvesting a field you already planted. You're returning to conversations that already have warmth in them.

Think about it through the training lens. An athlete doesn't wait to feel motivated before conditioning. The work gets done because it's scheduled and the payoff is real. Follow-up works the same way. One focused hour on warm deals, done consistently, will produce more results than an equivalent hour of cold outreach. The warm deals are already closer to the finish line.

The person who controls the conversation controls the outcome. You can't control a conversation you've already walked away from.

Your Real Quit Number

Before you finish this chapter, there's one number that belongs to you specifically.

What did your quit number cost you last year?

Take your graveyard. Estimate conservatively. Of the deals that got one or two touches and then went silent, what percentage might have closed if you'd shown up four or five more times with real value? Apply your average deal size to that estimate.

That number is the price tag on quitting early.

It's not a number to feel bad about. That's not the point. Guilt produces nothing useful. What you want is clarity, because clarity changes behavior in a way that regret never does.

When you know what walking away costs you, follow-up feels different. You stop thinking of it as a chore you owe the deal. You start seeing it as the most logical next move in your pipeline. The fifth conversation stops being awkward and starts being obvious. You're not chasing. You're returning to a conversation that wasn't finished yet.

Your competitors are quitting at touch two. Some quit at touch one. Some never followed up after the first call at all. They have their own graveyards, full of the same kinds of deals you have in yours.

The fifth conversation is the one they never got to.

It's available to you every time you're willing to show up for it.

Your Rep

The Drill. Pull your last 20 deals that went quiet. For each one, count the actual number of touches it received before you stopped reaching out. Write the number down next to each deal. Then ask one honest question for each: did they say no, or did you just stop asking? Find your real quit number before you close this chapter. This takes under an hour and it will change the way you read your pipeline.

The Questions. Use these as you work through each deal:

- "How many conversations did this deal actually get?"
- "Did they say no, or did I stop asking?"
- "What was this deal worth?"
- "What would one more conversation have cost me, and what might it have paid?"

Train It. The 90-day version of this drill is in The Fifth Conversation Workbook, at ConvoControl.com/fifthconversation.

Chapter Two

The Fear of Being Annoying

What are you actually afraid of when you don't make the call?

Not the surface answer. Not "I don't want to bother them." Go one level deeper. Sit with it for a second. What is the real thing?

Most sellers, when they finally get honest about it, land on the same answer. They're afraid of being seen as desperate. They're afraid the prospect will think less of them. They're afraid that reaching out again will reveal something about where they stand, and that something won't be flattering.

That fear is one of the three things that kill deals. No system. Nothing to say. Fear. And fear is the one that doesn't look like an enemy.

And what makes it so dangerous is that the fear feels completely reasonable. It masquerades as self-awareness. It sounds like respect for the prospect's time. It tells you a tidy story: you're not following up because you're being considerate, professional, polite.

But underneath that reasonable surface, it's just a story you're telling yourself so you don't have to make the call.

This chapter is about naming that story precisely, because named fears shrink. Unnamed fears run everything.

Name the Fear Precisely

There's a principle that runs through this entire approach: you can't train around something you haven't named. If you can't identify what's stopping you, you can't address it. You just keep stopping, over and over, while telling yourself it's the right call.

So let's put a precise name on this one.

The fear of being annoying is really the fear of lowering your status in someone else's eyes. You believe that following up signals need. And need, in a sales conversation, feels like the opposite of control. You don't want to look like you're waiting by the phone. You don't want the prospect to sense your hunger through a text message or an email subject line.

That's the actual fear. Status. Perception. The story about what your follow-up says about you.

And once you name it that clearly, something shifts. Because when you look at that fear straight on, you realize it's built on a flawed assumption: that your follow-up is about you.

A follow-up call isn't a statement about how badly you want the deal. It's a move in a conversation that you are responsible for keeping alive. The prospect didn't close the loop. You're closing it for both of you. That's not desperation. That's what professionals do.

Here's the other thing worth sitting with. When you don't follow up, you're making a decision on the prospect's behalf. You're deciding they've moved on. You're deciding they're not interested. You're deciding, without any evidence, that the deal is over. And you're doing all of that without ever asking.

That's not respect for their time. That's avoidance wearing a polite disguise.

Think about the deals sitting in your pipeline right now. The ones that went quiet. How many of them got a clear "no"? How many of them got silence that you interpreted as no, and then you honored that interpretation by going silent yourself?

Two silences. Neither one of them a real answer.

The fear of being annoying doesn't protect your prospects from discomfort. It protects you from the possibility of rejection. That's a very different thing, and it's worth being honest about.

Name the fear. It's status anxiety dressed up as consideration. Once you see it clearly, you can set it down and get back to the work you were hired to do.

There's a rep worth running right now, just mentally. Think of the last deal you stopped following up on. Go back to the exact moment you decided to stop. What were you telling yourself? Was it "they're clearly not interested"? Was it "I don't want to be pushy"? Was it "if they wanted to move forward, they would've called me"?

Every one of those is a story. None of them is confirmed evidence. The deal didn't close itself, and it didn't get a burial. It just got abandoned.

That's the pattern this book exists to break.

The Empathy Flip

Try this. Think about the last time a prospect went quiet on you. What was your first instinct about what the silence meant?

Most sellers go straight to rejection. "They're not interested." "They changed their mind." "Something I said killed it." The silence gets filled with a story, and the story is almost always the worst possible interpretation.

Now flip the camera. What was actually happening on their end?

They had a board presentation to prepare. Their biggest client sent a crisis email at 6 a.m. Their team lead went on vacation and left their inbox a disaster. Budget got frozen mid-quarter without warning. They had the conversation with you, then had five more conversations that day, then forgot where they put your proposal. They fully intended to follow up and just haven't gotten to it yet.

Silence doesn't mean no. Silence is a "not yet," not a "go away."

Where you are in the conversation matters. Silence after a first conversation is different from silence after a proposal. It can mean the prospect is still deciding whether the problem is worth solving. It can mean they're waiting on approval from someone above them. It can mean the timing is wrong for this quarter. That's not a decision against you.

Your follow-up is not the center of their day. It's a minor interruption in a packed calendar, and if it's actually useful, it gets a reply.

That reframe changes how you approach every single touch from two onward. You're not intruding. You're showing up for a conversation that you both started. You're the one keeping it alive because that's what the trained version of this job looks like.

Here's the test. When was the last time you were genuinely annoyed that someone followed up with you in a way that was actually useful? Not the same voicemail for the fourth time. Not the "just checking in" for the third week in a row. An actual useful message, arriving at a reasonable time, with something worth reading?

You probably answered that email. You probably appreciated it.

Real annoyance comes from repetition without value. It comes from the seller who didn't listen to anything you said, shows no evidence of remembering your situation, and keeps firing the same message at you on a schedule. That seller isn't being persistent. They're being lazy. There's a big difference.

A seller who shows up with something relevant, asks one real question, and respects the pace of your decision? That seller gets through.

The empathy flip isn't a mindset trick you apply once and forget. It's a standing calibration. Every time the fear shows up, every time you start telling yourself that reaching out again would be an imposition, run the flip. Ask yourself what's actually happening in their world. Ask whether you're reading silence correctly or projecting your own anxiety onto it.

The silence can be circumstance. And circumstances change.

Picture a rep, call him Marcus. Marcus had a strong first call with a facilities manager at a mid-size company. Great energy, great questions, the prospect even asked for a proposal. Two weeks passed with no response. Marcus started building a story. "Maybe the proposal was too high. Maybe they went with someone else. Maybe I should wait a bit longer so I don't seem too eager."

Three weeks in, Marcus finally sent a short follow-up. Not a "just checking in." He'd seen a piece about a local regulation change that affected facilities costs directly, and he mentioned it, then asked one question: "Did this come across your radar? It changes one of the numbers we talked about."

The reply came in two hours. The facilities manager had been stuck in a facilities audit that ate three weeks of his calendar. He hadn't forgotten the conversation. He'd just been buried. The relevant note gave him a reason to come up for air.

Marcus got the fifth conversation because he stopped asking whether to reach out and started asking what to bring when he did.

What Annoying Actually Is

Let's be precise. What actually makes a follow-up annoying?

Two things. Repetition without value. And pressure without permission.

Repetition without value is the follow-up that says nothing new. The "just checking in" message. The "any update?" text. The fourth voicemail that sounds exactly like the first three. The seller who reaches out seven times across two months with the same message, slightly rearranged, offering nothing useful and asking for nothing specific.

That is annoying. But notice what's actually causing the annoyance. It's not the frequency. It's the content. Or the total absence of it.

The prospect isn't irritated because you reached out. They're irritated because you reached out with nothing. Each empty touch spends a little more of the goodwill you built in the first conversation. You're making withdrawals without any deposits. By the fifth empty message, there's nothing left in the account.

The fix for repetition without value isn't fewer touches. It's better ones.

Pressure without permission is the second version. The manufactured urgency. The "I need a decision by end of week" email that has nothing real behind it. The fake deadline. The guilt-trip message that says "I've reached out several times without hearing back," which is basically using your own failure to provide value as a tool to make someone feel bad.

That's not persistence. That's emotional manipulation, and prospects can feel the difference.

Here's the cleaner version. Professional persistence looks like this: every touch gives something. A relevant insight. A question that moves the conversation an inch further. A piece of proof that speaks to their specific situation. A genuine check-in on something real that they mentioned in an earlier conversation.

Pests repeat themselves. Professionals advance the conversation.

Write that somewhere you'll see it. Because the moment you absorb it, the question changes. You stop asking yourself "should I reach out again?" and start asking "what's actually worth reaching out with?"

That is a far better question, and you can always answer it.

The difference shows up in the inbox immediately. Compare these two messages:

Message A: "Hi Sarah, just following up to see if you had a chance to review the proposal. Let me know when you'd like to connect."

Message B: "Hi Sarah, a company in your industry just dealt with the same onboarding bottleneck we talked about and cut their ramp time by restructuring one handoff. It's a quick read. Would it be useful if I sent it over?"

Message A is about the seller. It's asking for something with nothing attached. Message B is about Sarah. It's offering something and asking whether it's relevant.

One of those messages gets deleted. The other one gets a reply.

The training question is: which one do yours sound like?

Be honest. Go look at the last three follow-ups you sent. Pull them up right now if you can. Were they about you and the deal you need, or were they about the prospect and something useful to them?

If they were about you, you've found the actual problem. And now you can fix it.

The Permission Move

There's a technique that neutralizes most of the fear around follow-up before it gets a chance to take hold.

Ask for the follow-up while you're still in the conversation.

It sounds almost too straightforward. But it works because it restructures the relationship. Your next touch stops being an interruption. It becomes a kept promise. You stop wondering whether you're being intrusive and start showing up as exactly the professional you said you'd be.

Here's what it sounds like near the end of the first conversation, as things are wrapping up:

"Would it be okay if I checked back in two weeks? By then you'll have had time to bring this to your team, and I'll have some additional information that might be useful when you do."

They say yes, or they tell you when a better time would be. You asked a reasonable question in a reasonable way and gave a reasonable reason.

Now the second touch is entirely different. You're not reaching into someone's inbox uninvited. You're honoring something they agreed to. You're doing what you said you'd do. That's not annoying. That's reliable. And reliable is rare enough in sales that it stands out.

The rep who asks for the follow-up in the first conversation never has to talk themselves into making the second call. The permission is already there. The expectation is already set. All they're doing is showing up as promised.

You can build this into any conversation. "When would be a good time to check back in?" "Would it help if I sent a summary of what we covered in the next day or two?" "If I reach out next Thursday, is that too soon or about right?"

Each of those questions does two things at once. It schedules the next touch, and it gives you information about what the prospect actually wants from the follow-up process. Some people want weekly contact. Some need a month to talk internally. Some will tell you exactly what they'd need to see before they're ready to have another conversation.

Listen for all of it. The answers tell you exactly how to be useful instead of annoying.

The permission move is also a low-pressure way to surface real objections early. A prospect who is genuinely not interested will often tell you so when you ask directly and calmly. "Honestly, I don't think the timing works for us this year." That's not a bad outcome. That's a clear answer, and a clear answer is worth more than three weeks of silence you have to decode.

It frees up your attention for the deals that are real, and it keeps you out of the follow-up limbo that eats your calendar.

Make the permission question automatic. Ask it in every first conversation, every time. Not aggressively. Just naturally, as part of the close of the meeting. Turn it into a muscle-memory rep the way a strong closer turns every conversation into a natural next step. Do it enough times and it stops feeling like a technique. It just becomes how you work.

When the next touch is something you both agreed to, the fear of making it mostly disappears. You're not wondering if it's okay. You already know it is.

The Identity Shift

There's a deeper question underneath everything in this chapter, and it's worth sitting with for a moment.

Who are you in the follow-up?

A lot of sellers carry an identity that quietly works against them. They see themselves as the person asking for something. They're the one who wants the deal. They're the one who needs the yes. And from inside that identity, every follow-up feels like begging.

The shift that changes the whole experience is this: you're not the person asking for something. You're the person responsible for keeping a professional conversation alive until it reaches its natural conclusion.

You have something valuable. You know what it does. You've seen what it does for people who have similar problems to the person you're talking to. Your job is not to beg for an audience. Your job is to stay present, stay useful, and stay patient long enough for the timing to align and the decision to become clear.

Some deals need five conversations because the problem itself takes five conversations to fully understand. Some prospects need four touches before they trust you enough to be honest about what's actually holding things up. Some timing situations are real, the budget is genuinely not there yet, the system migration is genuinely still happening, and the deal is there, waiting, for whichever seller shows up when the calendar turns.

The person who keeps showing up, with something to offer each time, with patience and good questions and the right information at the right moment, is the person who gets there.

That person's identity is not "the rep chasing a deal." Their identity is "the professional who finishes what they start."

This comes up constantly in the ConvoDojo. Reps at every level, from six months in to fifteen years in, run into the same wall.

They have great first conversations. They build real rapport. And then something in them says "if they wanted this, they would've called back by now." And they stop.

That belief, buried in the identity, is a career limiter. It sounds like self-respect. It feels like not wanting to be pushy. But what it actually is, is a way to avoid the discomfort of persistence.

The most impressive first call doesn't close the deal. Staying in the deal does. Staying is the skill. Staying with something to offer every time is the trained version of that skill.

The identity you need is simple, and it has nothing to do with closing tricks or pressure tactics. It's this: you are a professional with something valuable, having a conversation with a peer who is busy and distracted and making real decisions that matter to their company. Your job is to be useful, patient, and persistent, in exactly that order.

The fear of being annoying is really just the fear of seeing yourself the wrong way. The pest follows up with nothing, hoping repetition will do what value couldn't. The professional follows up with something real, every time, until the conversation reaches its natural outcome.

You decide which one you are. And you decide it with every follow-up you send or don't send.

Most people read. Few people rep.

Reading this chapter tells you the difference between a pest and a professional. Repping it, sending the follow-up today on the deal you quietly abandoned last week, running the permission question in your next conversation, building the habit until the fear stops showing up for work, that's what actually changes your numbers.

The fifth conversation doesn't happen because you read about following up. It happens because you're still in the deal when everyone else already left it.

Your Rep

The Drill. Find the last deal you stopped following up on because you didn't want to seem pushy. Not the one that said no. The one you quietly let go. Locate it, whether it's in your CRM, your email, or a notebook. Write down one thing you could send today that would be genuinely useful to that person. A piece of information about their industry. A question based on something they mentioned in the first conversation. One thing with real value attached. Send it today. One message. No pitch. One question at the end.

The Questions. These are the reps to train with. Read them, adapt them to your voice and your market, and use them.

- "Would it be helpful if I sent over what we discussed, broken down for your team?"
- "When should I check back in so I'm actually useful instead of just noisy?"
- "What would need to change on your end for this to be worth another conversation?"
- "Would it be okay if I followed up in two weeks, once you've had time to bring this to the team?"
- "Is there something specific I could send that would make the next conversation worth your time?"

Train It. The 90-day version of this drill is in The Fifth Conversation Workbook, at ConvoControl.com/fifthconversation.

Chapter Three

Ask Questions. Stop Vomiting Information.

When someone goes quiet on you, what do you send? Be honest. Is it a question, or is it a brochure?

Most sellers send a brochure. Maybe not a literal one, but the digital equivalent. A long email. A PDF attachment. A bulleted list of every feature they forgot to mention on the first call. A link to a case study. Sometimes all four, wrapped in a subject line that says "More information as promised!" even when no one promised anything.

The prospect didn't ask for homework. They asked for nothing. They went quiet. And the natural human response, especially for someone whose job is to sell, is to fill that silence with content. More words, more proof, more reasons to buy. If they just understood the product better, they'd say yes. So you write more. You attach more. You explain more.

The prospect gets the email. They see the wall of text, the three attachments, the nested bullet points. They feel the weight of it. And they do what any busy person does with something that requires thirty minutes they don't have: they defer it. One more thing sitting at the bottom of a pile.

You didn't just fail to get a reply. You made yourself harder to deal with.

The Default Follow-Up Failure

The information dump is the default follow-up behavior because it feels like effort. It looks like you're working. You spent an hour on that email. You found a great article and attached it. You included the pricing matrix, the comparison chart, and the testimonials page. From the inside, it feels like due diligence. From the outside, it reads as noise.

Think about what an information dump actually requires of the prospect. They have to open it, read it, process it, decide what matters, and figure out how to respond. You gave them five jobs. They didn't ask for one. The mental cost is real, and when something feels like too much work, people don't do it. They wait. And waiting in sales means losing.

The flip side of the information dump is the question you never asked. That question is where the deal lives.

Every message you send is competing with everything else on that person's screen. Their boss's request from this morning. A Slack thread that won't stop. The meeting they're already five minutes late to. For your message to win even thirty seconds of focused attention, it has to be frictionless. A single, clear question is frictionless. A wall of features is the opposite.

Picture a rep, call him Marcus. He's in software sales. He runs a solid first call with a director at a mid-size company. The director seems interested, asks good questions, says he'll think it over. Marcus gets off the call and immediately drafts a follow-up. He adds the feature comparison sheet, links to three case studies, a note about the new integration capability, and a paragraph explaining the onboarding process. He spends forty-five minutes building it.

The director reads the subject line. Sees the attachments. Thinks "I'll get to this later." Later never comes.

Marcus follows up two weeks after that with another email. Same approach. More information. Another case study. A note that says "I just wanted to make sure you had everything you needed."

The director still doesn't reply. Marcus marks the deal dead and moves on.

What Marcus never sent was a question. One clean, direct question that gave the director something easy to answer. One question that would have kept the conversation alive without requiring an hour of reading. Marcus had a shot at the fifth conversation, and he buried it under a pile of content nobody asked for.

That pattern plays out in pipelines everywhere. And it's not because sellers are bad at their jobs. It's because nobody ever taught them that silence calls for a question, not a briefing.

There's also something worth naming about the psychology here. When you send a dense information package after someone goes quiet, you're making an assumption about why they went quiet. You're assuming they don't have enough information. That assumption is almost always wrong. Often, buyers who go quiet aren't missing features. They're wrestling with timing, internal alignment, budget conversations, or competing priorities. More information doesn't fix any of those problems. A question that finds out which one it is does.

Why Questions Work

So why does a question cut through when information doesn't? It comes down to what each one requires.

Information asks the other person to receive, process, evaluate, and decide what to do with it. A question asks for one thing: an answer. Most people, especially in a professional context, feel some pull to respond when someone asks them something directly. It's social wiring. A question creates a conversational opening. A block of information closes one.

A well-placed question also hands the conversational ball back to the prospect. When you send a question, the ball is in their court. There's a gentle social expectation attached to it. They don't have to answer, but it registers when they don't. A question stays open. An information dump closes with a period.

Questions give you signal, too. When a prospect answers, you learn something. Where the deal actually stands. What they're thinking about. What's slowing them down. When a prospect receives information and doesn't respond, you learn nothing. You're guessing at the obstacle while they drift further away.

There's a practical mechanics reason as well. A question is small. It fits in two lines. It doesn't demand thirty minutes. It fits between a Slack message and a meeting. The barrier to responding is low, and low barriers get cleared.

Think about the messages you actually reply to when your own inbox is overloaded. You don't fight through the long ones first. You clear the easy ones. The two-liners. The ones that just need a yes or a no. Questions get through because they're manageable.

That's the trade you want to make. Take your information, condense it to the single most important thing you want the prospect to engage with, and turn that into one question. One. The rest of the information can wait. It'll matter a lot more once the conversation is alive again.

The question also does something subtler. A question implies a relationship. When you ask someone something, you're treating them as a thinking person with a perspective worth hearing. When you send them information, you're treating them as a recipient. One of those postures opens doors. The other one builds walls.

You want to be the person who asks. That's the whole game in follow-up, just like it is in the room.

The Autopsy

Let's take five messages that flood inboxes every day and cut them open. You've probably sent at least three of these. You've definitely received all five.

"Just checking in."

This one is at the top of every list of bad follow-ups, and it deserves its spot. It contains no question, no value, and no reason to respond.

Rewritten: "Has the problem we talked about gotten louder or quieter since then?"

That question does what "just checking in" never could. It references the real issue. It invites a real answer. It respects the prospect's situation and asks them about it directly. The person on the other end reads it and has to think for a second. That's what you want. You want to be the message that made them think.

The info dump with three attachments.

You know this one. The follow-up email that's longer than the original proposal. Case studies. A PDF. A link to a video. A comparison chart. A paragraph explaining something you already explained on the call. Sent with good intentions and received as a burden.

The reason this fails is the same reason a pop quiz fails: it puts the burden on the other person before they've agreed to pick it up. You're asking someone who hasn't said yes to a second conversation to do the homework you assigned from the first one. Most of them won't.

Rewritten: "Which part of what we covered is still worth exploring for your team, and which part fell flat?"

That question takes thirty seconds to answer. And it gives you exactly the information you need to know how to proceed. The prospect tells you what matters and what doesn't. You suddenly know what the next conversation should be about. That's worth more than any attachment you could send.

The guilt trip.

"I haven't heard back from you and just wanted to follow up."

Rewritten: "Is this still worth a conversation, or has the timing changed on your end?"

Clean. Respectful. Puts the decision in their hands without any emotional weight attached. They can say yes, they can say no, or they can say "actually, something shifted, let's talk." All three of those answers move the deal somewhere. None of them require guilt to work.

The fake urgency.

"Prices go up Friday!" "This offer expires at end of quarter!" "Last chance to lock in this rate!" If it's real urgency, lead with it honestly and back it up. If it's manufactured urgency designed to pressure someone into moving, the prospect can smell it immediately, and it destroys trust faster than almost anything else you can do.

Fake urgency is a shortcut that makes you feel like you're creating momentum. What it actually creates is skepticism. The prospect who gets the "prices go up Friday" email on a Thursday, and then gets the same email again the following Thursday, knows exactly what you're doing. And they trust you less for it.

You don't need fake urgency. You have a real problem they're trying to solve and a real conversation that already started. Use that.

Rewritten: "You mentioned the Q3 budget review is coming up. Does it make sense to get the numbers in front of you before then?"

Real timing. Real context. A question that serves them. That's what creates actual urgency, because it's tied to something happening in their world, not something you invented in yours.

The theatrical breakup email.

Everyone copied this from the same blog post sometime around 2018. "I've tried to reach you several times and haven't heard back, so I'll assume you're not interested. I'll close out your file. If things change, feel free to reach out." It's meant to provoke a response by threatening withdrawal. Sometimes it does. More often, it burns a bridge you'd have rather kept.

The breakup approach can work, but not as theater. Chapter 13 covers the real version, which starts with a question and leaves the door open with grace. The theatrical version just ends the relationship and calls it a tactic.

Rewritten: "Should I close the file on this, or is there still a conversation worth having?"

One question. Honest. Direct. Gives them a clear path without the drama. And if the deal is dead, you find out. If it isn't, you just saved it.

The pattern in every rewrite is the same. A question replaces content. It's shorter. It's clearer. It demands less and gets more. Every time.

The One-Question Rule

One question per touch. Not two. Not five. One.

Two questions split attention. The prospect reads both and answers neither, or answers the easier one and ignores the one that matters. Five questions turn a follow-up into a survey, and surveys have low completion rates for a reason. They feel like a project. They signal that the sender hasn't done the work of figuring out what the deal actually needs right now.

One question forces discipline. It forces you to decide what the most important thing is at this exact moment. What do you need to know to move this deal forward? What's the single thing, if answered, that changes the next conversation? Find that. Ask only that.

This is harder than it sounds. When you sit down to write a follow-up, you probably have three things you want to know and four things you want to say. The temptation is to pack all of it in. The discipline is to pick one.

Pick the question that unlocks everything else. Ask it. Leave space for the answer. The other questions can wait for the next conversation, which you'll have because this one got answered.

The one-question rule also makes your training measurable. If every touch has one question, you can see whether the questions you're asking are actually working. Did that question get answered? Did it move the deal? Did it surface something you didn't know? When you spray five questions at once, you can't measure anything. When you ask one, you can see exactly what's working. That data builds over time. You get sharper at picking the right question for the right moment.

Think about what happens at the other end. The prospect gets your message. One question. That's it. They read it in ten seconds. They think about the answer. They type it. Done. The friction is low enough that responding feels easy. And they hit send. That's the fifth conversation starting up again from a dead stop, and all it took was one question instead of five paragraphs.

Some sellers worry that one question seems too simple. Too short. Like they're not taking the relationship seriously. Flip that. The discipline to ask only what matters is a sign of respect. It says "I know your time is valuable, so I'm not going to waste it." That posture tells a prospect something about how you operate. And how you show up in the small moments is how they imagine you'll show up in the big ones.

One more thing. The one-question rule applies to the message, not to your thinking. Before you write the question, you should know what a yes answer means, what a no answer means, and what you'll do with each. The question is one. The preparation behind it doesn't have to be.

Open vs. Closed

Every question you ask falls into one of two categories, and knowing which one to use, and when, separates a seller who advances deals from one who just stays in touch.

Open questions invite explanation. They start with what, how, who, or where. They're the questions you ask when you want dialogue. When you want to understand what's happening. When the deal is still alive and you need information. "What's changed since we talked?" is open. "How did the team react when you brought it up?" is open. "What would make the next step easier?" is open.

Open questions get people talking. And when people talk, they tell you things. Where the hesitation actually lives. Who else is involved in the decision. What they're comparing you against. What their boss is worried about. None of that comes out in response to a closed question. It comes out when you give someone room to think out loud. The Questions Close Deals system is built around this insight: genuine curiosity lowers defenses. When a prospect feels heard rather than pitched at, they're more likely to stop managing what they say and start thinking out loud. And thinking out loud is often where the real information lives.

Closed questions demand a decision. They start with did, is, are, will, or have. They're the questions you use when you need a binary answer. When you've gathered enough information and now you need clarity. "Is this still a priority?" is closed. "Did the board approve the budget?" is closed. "Are we moving forward?" is closed.

Closed questions create clarity. They cut through ambiguity. A deal that's been sitting in a warm holding pattern for three weeks sometimes just needs one direct closed question to land somewhere. Closed questions are how you get a deal off the fence.

The mistake most sellers make is asking the wrong type at the wrong time. They ask closed questions too early, when they don't have enough information yet, and they get a "not yet" that shuts the conversation down before it had a chance to open. Or they ask open questions too late, when what the deal needs is a decision, and they get more information when what they needed was movement.

The general flow looks like this. Early in a stalled deal, use open questions. You want dialogue. You want to understand what's happening on their side. You need real information before you can do anything useful with it. Mid-deal, when you have some information and you're working toward clarity, mix them. Late-deal, when the options are clear and the decision just needs to land, go closed. Clean. Direct. Respectful.

One thing to watch: open questions can feel softer, but they're not always the safer choice. Sometimes a prospect uses the room you gave them to explain why they're going in a different direction. That's still useful. You'd rather have the real answer than stay in the dark for another month. Closed questions can feel blunter, but they're often kinder. They give the other person permission to say no clearly, which ends the limbo and lets both of you move on.

Most sellers lean too hard on one type and avoid the other. If you tend to ask a lot of open questions and deals stay warm but never move, you probably need more closed ones late in the cycle. If you tend to rush to decisions before you understand the situation, you probably need more open ones early.

Watch the pattern in your own follow-ups. Are your deals dying for lack of information, or dying because you never asked for a decision? The type of question you lead with tells you which side of that problem you're on.

Questions are the only tool in follow-up that do both jobs: they advance a deal when it's alive, and they give you clarity when it isn't. Use them with intention.

Your Rep

The Drill. Take your three most-used follow-up templates and rewrite each one down to a single question. Then pick one deal that's been quiet for at least a week and send it a single open question today.

The Questions.

"Has the problem we talked about gotten louder or quieter since then?"

"What did your team say when you brought it up?"

"Is this still on the list for this quarter, or has it moved?"

"What would make the next conversation worth your time?"

"If there's one thing holding this up, what is it?"

Train It. The 90-day version of this drill is in The Fifth Conversation Workbook, at ConvoControl.com/fifthconversation.

Chapter Four

Follow-Up Is Control, Not Chasing

Who's controlling this deal right now, you or your voicemail box?

Sit with that for a second. You had a solid first conversation. The prospect was engaged. They asked good questions. They said they'd think about it. And now you're waiting. Refreshing your email. Wondering if you should call. Talking yourself out of calling. Drafting a message and deleting it. Drafting it again.

While you're doing all that, the deal is sitting still. And sitting still, in sales, means dying slowly.

Here's what most sellers get wrong about follow-up: they think about it as a favor they're asking for. They're hoping the prospect will give them a little of their time, a little of their attention, maybe a yes. That "hoping" posture shows up in everything they write and say. And the prospect reads it immediately, even through a screen.

Control feels different from chasing. And you can learn the difference. You can train it.

Define the Difference

Let's get specific about what these two things actually look like, because the line between them matters more than most sellers realize.

Chasing is when the prospect holds the conversation and you beg for it back. Every message you send is a plea. You need their attention. You need their decision. You need them to respond so you can stop feeling anxious about the deal. The energy under every touch is scarcity. You're waiting for permission to move forward.

Control looks completely different. Every touch you send puts something in their hands, usually a question, that is easier to answer than to ignore. You own the frame. You set the timeline. You decide when the next conversation happens, or at least you make the ask for it. The energy under every touch is confidence. You have something valuable and you're offering it to a peer.

Picture a rep, call him Marcus. Marcus has been chasing a mid-sized company for three months. He emails them every two weeks. The subject line says "Following up" or "Checking in" or "Just wanted to circle back." He waits. He wonders. He sends another. At no point does Marcus own any part of the process. He's entirely at the mercy of whenever they decide to respond.

Now picture a different version of Marcus, trained version. He sends a message with one specific question tied to something real in the prospect's world. He closes every email with a proposed next step. When the prospect doesn't reply, he doesn't send a carbon copy of the last message. He changes channels, changes the question, and stays calm. He doesn't need this deal to close today. He knows the fifth conversation is still ahead, and he's managing his way toward it deliberately.

Same deal. Same prospect. Completely different posture. One Marcus is chasing. The other is controlling.

The difference isn't about being pushy or passive. It isn't about volume of touches or how long you wait between them. The difference is whether you own the next step or wait for someone to hand it back to you.

Chasing surrenders the next move. Control keeps it.

When you're chasing, the prospect can ghost you without consequence. They feel no pull back into the conversation because you've handed over all the momentum. When you control the conversation, they have something to respond to. A question sitting in someone's inbox creates a gentle but real pull. A "just checking in" creates nothing. It demands their energy and offers none.

The Core Law Applied After the Room

In Questions Close Deals, the foundation was this: the person who controls the conversation controls the outcome. That law doesn't stop at the door when the first meeting ends. It runs the entire length of a deal, from the first hello to the signed agreement. It just operates on a longer clock after the room.

In the room, control is built through questions. You ask, they answer, and the conversation moves in the direction your questions lead it. You steer without forcing. You guide without pressuring. The prospect feels heard and understood, not pushed. That's the system.

The moment you walk out the door, most sellers abandon that system completely. They go from skilled, question-led conversationalists to people who write emails that say "hope this finds you well" and wait. They traded control for politeness, and their pipeline shows it.

The same tool that works in the room works in every follow-up touch. A question. One well-placed question shifts the conversational ball back to the prospect, keeps the dialogue open, and anchors your next step to their reality. After the room, questions don't close deals in a single message. But they keep you in the conversation long enough to get to the moment where the deal can close.

A question preserves the prospect's ability to respond and lets you guide the next move. It gives them a third option: answer this specific thing. That's a much lower ask than "make a decision." It keeps the door open when it would otherwise close quietly.

After the room, you're on a longer clock. Deals that take five or more conversations to close don't happen because someone kept pitching. They happen because someone kept asking. They kept the conversation alive with one question at a time, one touch at a time, until the prospect's situation shifted enough for a yes to be possible.

The fifth conversation doesn't happen by accident. It happens because somebody owned every step between conversation one and conversation five.

The Chase-Language Audit

Words signal status. Every word you choose in a follow-up message tells the prospect exactly where you see yourself in relation to them. And the most common follow-up words in sales broadcast one thing clearly: I'm below you, I need you, please respond.

Let's look at the specific words and phrases that give away control. You've written these before. Most sellers have.

"Just." This tiny word does enormous damage. "I just wanted to follow up." "I just had a quick question." "Just checking in to see how things are going." Every "just" is a shrink. It minimizes you. It apologizes for your presence. It signals that you know you're a bother and you're trying to take up as little space as possible. Remove every "just" from your follow-up vocabulary. Nothing you send is "just" anything. You have something valuable and a real question worth asking.

"Sorry to bother you." If you're sorry to bother them, why are you doing it? This phrase creates the exact dynamic you're trying to avoid. You've framed your follow-up as an interruption before you've even said what you wanted to say. The prospect now reads everything after it through that lens. Skip the apology. A peer doesn't apologize for reaching out. A peer reaches out because they have something worth saying.

"I know you're busy, but..." This one is tricky because it sounds considerate. And in conversation, acknowledging someone's time constraints is good manners. But in a follow-up email, this phrase operates as a submission signal. You're pre-emptively accepting that your message might not be worth their time. If you didn't believe your message was worth their time, you shouldn't send it. If you do believe it's worth their time, send it without the qualifier.

"Whenever you get a chance." This phrase is a timeless killer. It removes all urgency and all structure from the follow-up. It tells the prospect that there's no real next step here, no real reason to respond by any particular time, no actual ask. "Whenever you get a chance" will never be answered because "whenever" never arrives for busy people. It gets filed in the back of the mental drawer and forgotten.

"I haven't heard back from you..." Covered in Chapter 3, but worth noting here in the context of control. This phrase is the guilt trip, and guilt trips are the opposite of peer behavior. You're not their parent.

You're not owed a response by the date you decided to send the email. A peer checks in because they have something useful. A supplicant checks in because they haven't been acknowledged.

Now here's what each of those rewrites looks like in peer language.

"Just wanted to follow up" becomes a specific question. "You mentioned the timeline was Q4. Is that still holding?" Short. Direct. No apology for your existence.

"Sorry to bother you, but I wanted to touch base" becomes "Two things changed in the market this week that are worth a quick look for your situation. Want the short version?" Confident. Specific. Gives them a reason to reply.

"I know you're busy, but whenever you get a chance" becomes "Thursday at 2 or Friday morning, which works better?" Specific. Actionable. Treats both of you as professionals with schedules.

The goal isn't to sound aggressive or demanding. The goal is to sound like someone who knows what they're doing and has something worth talking about. That's it. That's the whole reframe.

Read your last ten sent follow-ups right now. Read them the way your prospect reads them. Count the "justs." Count the apologies. Count the times you said "whenever" or "if you have time" or "no rush." Every one of those is a moment where you handed the conversation over to someone who didn't want it and wasn't waiting for it.

Peer language isn't cold. It isn't rude. It's just clear. Clear questions. Clear next steps. Clear reason to respond.

Posture

Everything in the last section is about words, but the words are a symptom. The root cause is posture. What do you believe about your value, your role, and your relationship to the prospect?

If you believe you're interrupting them, you'll write "sorry to bother you."

If you believe your product or service is a burden they might not want, you'll add three paragraphs explaining why it might not be a fit just to soften the ask.

If you believe the deal is yours to lose and they're doing you a favor by considering you, you'll write follow-ups that beg instead of lead.

Posture is the set of beliefs running under every message you send. And the prospect picks it up. Not because they're analyzing your word choices, though sometimes they are. They pick it up because human beings are wired to read status signals instantly, the same way you know within seconds whether a stranger approaching you on the street is confident or nervous.

Here's the posture that serves you in follow-up: you are a professional with something valuable, talking to a peer.

Sit with that. A professional with something valuable. You aren't showing up hat in hand hoping they'll let you in. You aren't apologizing for existing in their inbox. You have something real, and you've done the work to understand how it connects to their specific situation.

Talking to a peer. They're not above you. You're not beneath them. They're busy, and so are you. They have problems, and you have solutions that are genuinely relevant. This is a professional conversation between two people deciding together if working together makes sense.

That posture changes the energy of every message you send. It changes your subject lines. It changes how you open. It changes whether you end with "let me know if you have any questions" or with a specific ask and a proposed date.

Here's a useful test. Before you send any follow-up, read it and ask: does this sound like someone who believes they have something valuable to offer? Or does it sound like someone who's hoping to be allowed into the conversation?

If you can't answer yes to the first one, rewrite it.

The prospect isn't looking for a vendor who desperately needs their business. They're looking for someone who can actually help them. Those are two very different versions of you, and the words you choose signal which one showed up.

Posture is a trainable thing. It gets built through reps the same way any athletic skill gets built. You do the language audit. You rewrite the messages. You train yourself out of the apology phrases and into the peer questions. Over time, the peer posture becomes default. You stop writing "just" because you've trained yourself past it. You stop saying "I know you're busy" because you've replaced it with a habit that serves you better.

You don't rise to the occasion in a sales conversation. You fall back on how you've trained. The training here is replacing low-status habits with high-status ones, one follow-up at a time.

Control Is Structural

This is where a lot of people get confused. They think control is tonal. They think if they just sound more confident, or use firmer language, or project more authority, they'll feel less like they're chasing. That's the wrong place to look.

Tone matters, and posture matters, but control is actually built through structure. It comes from three places: owning the next step, owning the cadence, and owning the content. All three are coming in the chapters ahead. Here's a preview so you understand how they fit together.

Owning the next step is the highest-leverage habit in this book. Every conversation ends with the next conversation booked. Not "I'll follow up next week." Thursday at 2, you'll have the board's answer, I'll bring the updated numbers. A next conversation agreed to inside the room is worth ten follow-ups chased after. When you own the next step, you never have to ask if it's okay to follow up. It's already on the calendar.

Owning the cadence means knowing when to touch each deal and how often. The skill is placing each deal on the right rung and moving it deliberately, never vanishing. When you own the cadence, you're never improvising about whether to reach out. The system decides. You execute.

Owning the content means every touch delivers something real, a question, an insight, a piece of proof, something that gives the prospect a genuine reason to respond. Chapters 8 through 12 build this toolkit. When you own the content, you're never staring at a blank message wondering what to say. You have a value bank. You have question depth charts. You have a playbook for every stage of a deal.

When all three are working together, follow-up stops feeling like chasing. You're not waiting for a response. You're executing a sequence that was designed to get you to the fifth conversation. Each touch is deliberate. Each question has a purpose. Each cadence decision serves the deal.

That's the structure. That's what control looks like when it's fully built.

Right now, you might only have pieces of it. That's fine. Most sellers learn the structure in stages. The language audit in this chapter gives you the immediate fix: stop handing over status with your words.

The chapters ahead give you the longer build: a system where every element of follow-up serves your pipeline instead of draining it.

What matters right now is the shift in how you think about this. Follow-up is not a chore you perform while hoping for mercy. It's a trained sequence you execute from a place of confidence. Each touch is a move. Each question is a tool. Each booked next step is a victory.

Control is the skill. Chasing is the default. And defaults only stay defaults until you train past them.

Your Rep

The Drill. Pull up your last ten sent follow-up messages right now. Read every one of them looking for chase language. "Just." "Sorry to bother you." "I know you're busy." "Whenever you get a chance." "I haven't heard back." Count how many appear across those ten messages. Then rewrite each one. Same message, same intent, but in peer language: a clear question, a specific ask, a reason for them to respond. All ten rewrites should take you under an hour.

The Questions.

"Where does this leave us?"

"What's the next step you want to take?"

"Should we put a date on that?"

"What would it be useful for me to bring to the next conversation?"

"Is this still moving on your end, or has something shifted?"

Train It. The 90-day version of this drill is in The Fifth Conversation Workbook, at ConvoControl.com/fifthconversation.

Chapter Five

Why "No For Now" Is an Appointment

What did you do with the last "call me in a few months" you got? Where is it written down?

If your honest answer is "I'm not sure" or "I think I remember it," that deal is already gone. Not lost. Gone. There's a difference. Lost means someone beat you. Gone means you handed it away with both hands and walked off without noticing.

This chapter is about stopping that.

The stall is one of the most misread moments in sales. Most sellers hear a stall and feel the conversation closing. The energy drops. The prospect says something like "we just need a little more time" or "let's revisit this next quarter," and the untrained ear translates that into rejection. The deal goes into a mental pile labeled "not interested" and stays there until the CRM auto-archives it six months later.

But that's not what a stall is.

A stall is an appointment wearing street clothes. It has a trigger buried inside it and a timeline hidden in the words. Your job is to find both, write them down, and show back up exactly when you said you would. That's the whole skill. And almost nobody does it.

Stalls as Disguised Follow-Ups

Every stall contains two pieces of information. The first is what has to change before they can move. The second is when that change is likely to happen.

Most sellers catch neither.

"Call me in Q3" sounds like a brush-off. Trained sellers hear it as a date and a signal. Q3 means something specific to that prospect. Maybe it's when their fiscal year resets. Maybe it's when the board reviews the budget. Maybe it's when a current contract expires. You don't know yet, but the information is in the room if you ask one more question before you leave.

"We need to think about it" is the stall that frustrates sellers the most. It feels formless. There's no date, no trigger, no obvious way back in. But "we need to think about it" almost always has something underneath it. A stakeholder who hasn't weighed in. A concern that didn't get named in the conversation. A comparison they want to make. A number they need to justify. The stall is the surface. The real thing is underneath, and the only way to find it is to ask.

"Budget's frozen until January" is the clearest stall of all. January is a date. Frozen budget is the trigger. The only question is whether you write those two things down before you walk out the room or whether you let them evaporate.

Here's what separates the rep who closes from the rep who doesn't. When the stall lands, the closer leans in. They get curious. They ask the one or two questions that turn a vague "not now" into a specific "here's what has to happen and here's when." Then they log it. Then they leave the room knowing exactly when to come back and exactly what to say.

The stall is not a door closing. It's a door that's slightly ajar, with a sign on it that says "knock after October." The rep who reads that sign and shows up in October gets the deal. The rep who read it as a rejection doesn't.

From this point in the book, every stall you encounter is a follow-up in disguise. Your job is to decode it before the conversation ends.

The Follow-Up File

This is the system that catches what your memory drops.

Memory is a terrible pipeline manager. You walk out of five calls on a Tuesday with five different stalls, each one wearing different clothing, each one with a different timeline and a different trigger. By Thursday you remember two of them clearly. By next week you remember the feeling that some things are still out there somewhere. By next month, your CRM shows five dead deals and you have no idea what happened.

The follow-up file fixes this. It's not complicated. It's three columns and a reflex.

For every stall, you log three things before the next conversation starts.

The first is the trigger. The trigger is what they said has to change before they can move. It's the condition. "Budget opens." "Migration completes." "Partner signs off." "New fiscal year starts." "We see how Q3 lands." Write the trigger in their words, or as close to their words as you can get. This matters later.

The second is the date. The date is when the trigger is due. Sometimes they give you an exact one: "Call me after the 15th." More often it's approximate: "sometime in the fall" or "once things settle down." When it's approximate, nail it down before you leave. Ask one more question. "When in the fall are we thinking? Early October, or closer to November?" You want a date on the calendar, not a season in your head.

The third is your reopen question. This is the question you'll ask when you come back. You write it now, while the conversation is fresh, not four months later when you've forgotten everything about this deal. The reopen question quotes their words back to them and confirms whether the trigger happened. You'll see exactly how this works in the examples below.

That's the whole system. Three columns. Trigger, date, question. Fill them in before you close the call or immediately after. Don't let a day pass. The longer you wait, the less you remember and the more you'll paraphrase instead of quote. Paraphrases are forgettable. Their exact words are not.

What tool you use doesn't matter. Your CRM, a notebook, a calendar note on the date they gave you, a sticky note on your monitor. The tool is not the point. The logging reflex is. The moment a stall lands, the reflex fires: trigger, date, question. That's what you train.

The Re-Open Technique

Four months pass. The date arrives. You open your follow-up file, find the entry, and see the trigger, the date, and the question you wrote in the room.

Now what?

You send the question. Exactly as written. In their words.

This is the re-open technique, and it works for a reason that has nothing to do with being clever. When someone hears their own words reflected back to them, they can't mistake it for a mass email. There is no sequence, no automation, no AI assistant on the planet that knows what that specific person said in that specific conversation. Only you know. And the fact that you know it, remembered it, and came back on the date you promised tells them something important about you before they even read the question.

It tells them you were paying attention.

"Last time we talked, you said budget opens in October. Did it?"

That's it. That's the entire message. No preamble. No re-pitching. No "I wanted to circle back and reconnect to discuss how our solutions might align with your evolving needs." Just their words, confirmed or not.

Here's why short works better than long. The prospect hasn't been thinking about you for four months. You have been thinking about them, or at least your system has. When you re-appear, their brain needs a second to reorient. A long message demands more from a brain that's still catching up. A short, specific question they can answer in ten seconds? That lands.

Two additional reasons this technique holds up. First, it's completely honest. You're not manufacturing urgency or inventing a reason to reach out. The reason is real: they gave you a timeline and you're honoring it. That's professional behavior, and prospects notice. Second, it hands them something easy to respond to. "Did the budget open?" has two possible answers. Yes or no. Either one starts a conversation. Either one is better than silence.

The one failure mode to avoid: using their words as a trick. This isn't manipulation. It's memory. The goal is to have a real conversation about whether their situation changed and whether your solution still makes sense. If the trigger didn't happen, you find out why, log a new date, and come back again. If it did happen, you pick up right where you left off.

The person who controls the conversation controls the outcome. Quoting their own words back to them puts you in control of the re-open without a single drop of pressure.

Three Worked Examples

Let's walk three common stalls from the moment they land to the moment you re-enter. These are composite examples built from the patterns that show up across every industry. Adapt the language to your market.

The Q3 Budget Stall

You're in a conversation with a prospect, call her Renee, who runs a mid-size distribution company. She likes what she heard. The problem is real. But when you ask about moving forward, she says: "We just don't have budget allocated for this right now. It frees up at the start of Q3."

Before you leave, you ask: "When does Q3 start for you? Is that July 1, or does your fiscal year run differently?"

She confirms: first week of July.

Your log entry looks like this.

Trigger: Budget frees up at the start of Q3 (July 1). Date: First week of July. Question: "You mentioned budget opens first week of July. Is that still the timeline, or did things shift?"

You schedule a task for June 25, a few days early so you're not scrambling. When the date arrives, you send the question. Short. Specific. In her words.

Renee reads it and either confirms the budget opened, in which case you schedule a call, or she tells you there was a delay, in which case you get a new date and log it again. Either outcome is a conversation. Either one keeps the deal alive.

The "We're Switching Systems First" Stall

Picture a rep named Marcus who sells an analytics platform. He's talking to a VP of operations who's genuinely interested but says: "We can't layer on anything new until we finish migrating to the new ERP. We're about six to eight weeks from done."

Marcus asks: "What does done look like for you? Is there a go-live date you're working toward?"

The VP says they're targeting the end of the month, six weeks out.

Log entry:

Trigger: ERP migration completes (go-live at end of month, six weeks). Date: Six weeks from today. Question: "You were mid-migration when we last talked. Is the dust settled enough to take another look?"

Marcus sets a reminder for week seven, giving one week of buffer for things to settle. When he reaches out, he doesn't pitch. He asks the question. If the migration hit a snag, he gets an update and a new window. If it finished, he has a reason to re-engage that the VP himself created.

Notice what Marcus didn't do: he didn't send four follow-up emails in the six weeks asking "any update on the migration?" That would be noise. One message at the right moment, using the trigger the VP provided, is the entire move.

The "Let Me Talk to My Partner" Stall

This one feels soft, but it has teeth if you handle it right. A prospect, call him David, is a small business owner considering a service you sell. He says: "I need to run this by my business partner before we can commit. We make all major decisions together."

Before you end the call, you ask two things. First: "When do you think you'll have a chance to sit down with him?" David says probably later that week, maybe by Friday. Second: "Is there anything specific he'll want to know that we didn't cover today? I want to make sure you have what you need to have that conversation."

That second question is important. It helps David prepare, and it tells you what the real objection might be hiding behind the partner.

Log entry:

Trigger: Partner conversation happens (David said by Friday). Date: The following Monday. Question: "You were going to talk to your partner by Friday. How did that go?"

One week later, Monday morning, you send the question. If David talked to his partner and the answer is yes, you book the next call. If he didn't get to it yet, you find out why and get a new window. If the partner said no, David tells you, and now you have real information to work with.

Every one of these scenarios is a real conversation. That's the goal. You're not trying to manipulate David into a yes. You're trying to keep the conversation alive long enough to find out whether the answer is actually yes, no, or not yet.

The Mindset Close

Here's the reframe that makes this whole system click into place.

A stall is not a rejection you survived. It's an invitation you accepted. When someone says "call me in three months," they're telling you exactly what you need to know. Every "no for now" you log and return to is a deal that's still alive. It doesn't matter that the clock is running slowly. Slow deals close. They close for the rep who shows back up and nobody else.

This is where the fifth conversation lives. Your competitors had the first one. Maybe two or three of them made a follow-up attempt. By the time you're showing back up in month three, month four, or month seven with the prospect's own words in hand and a specific question that proves you've been paying attention, you're the only person still in the room. Not because you were more persistent in some annoying, relentless way. Because you had a system and they didn't.

Think about what you're actually competing against. The other sellers who talked to this prospect probably had one conversation and sent one or two vague follow-up emails. Then they moved on. They left the deal in a CRM labeled "stalled" and let the software archive it. You logged the trigger. You wrote the question. You set the date. And when the date arrived, you showed up.

That's not a hustle story. That's a training story.

You don't rise to the occasion in a high-stakes follow-up moment. You fall back on how you've trained. If you've trained the habit of logging every stall before you leave the room, then showing up in October with the right question is automatic. If you haven't trained it, you'll be staring at a dead deal in October wondering what you said to that person six months ago.

The habit is trainable. The reflex is buildable. And the cost of building it is about thirty seconds per conversation. That's the log entry. Thirty seconds in the room, months of pipeline value on the back end.

One more thing worth naming. The rep who comes back on the date they promised is the rep the prospect trusts. Trust is built through small, consistent demonstrations of competency. You said you'd call in October. You called in October. That's rare. That's memorable. And it sets the tone for every conversation that follows. By the time you get to the fifth conversation, you're not a vendor. You're the person who does what they say they're going to do. In sales, that's worth more than any pitch ever written.

Build the file. Log the trigger. Set the date. Write the question. Come back. Every stall you handle this way is a door you left open. Every one you don't is a door you closed yourself and handed the key to whoever shows up next.

Your Rep

The Drill.

Go through your CRM, your notebook, your email, or wherever you keep deal notes. Find five "no for now" deals. For each one, ask yourself whether you got a stall before the silence started. If you did, write down the trigger and the timeline, even if you have to reconstruct them from memory. Then write the reopen question in their words. Set a dated reminder for each one. Do this before you put this book down today.

If you can't remember what the stall was, that's your data. That's what a missing log entry costs you. Use that feeling as motivation to run the three-column log on every deal from this point forward.

The Questions.

"Last time you told me budget opens in October. Did it?"

"You wanted to see how the Q3 numbers came in. What did they tell you?"

"You were mid-migration when we talked. Is the dust settled enough to pick this back up?"

"You said you'd talk to your partner by the end of the week. How did that go?"

"When we spoke in the spring, timing was the issue. Has anything shifted?"

Train It.

The 90-day version of this drill is in The Fifth Conversation Workbook, at ConvoControl.com/fifthconversation.

Chapter Six

Never Leave Without the Next Conversation

What's the last question you ask before any sales conversation ends? Think about your last five calls. What were your actual closing words?

If you're like most sellers, the answer sounds something like "I'll follow up with you," or "Let me know if you have any questions," or the classic "Talk soon." Warm enough. Friendly enough. And completely worthless for keeping the deal alive.

Because what you said at the end of that conversation is now in control of what happens next. And "talk soon" is not a plan. It's a wish.

This chapter is about one habit. Just one. But if you install it and nothing else from this book sticks, you'll still come out ahead of most of the competition. The habit is this: every single sales conversation ends with the best version of a next step that the moment allows, ideally a booked conversation.

Before the call wraps. Before you close the tab. Before you walk to your car in the parking lot. The next conversation is on the calendar.

That's the whole thing. Let's talk about how to make it happen every time.

The Single Highest-Leverage Habit

Picture a rep, call him Marcus. He runs a solid first call. The prospect is engaged, asks good questions, seems genuinely interested. At the end, Marcus says, "Great talking with you. I'll send over some info and follow up next week." The prospect says, "Sounds good." They hang up.

Now Marcus is in follow-up mode. He sends an email Tuesday. No reply. He sends another Thursday. No reply. He calls Friday and leaves a voicemail. Nothing. A week goes by and he's already moved from "confident this is a live deal" to "should I even bother?"

What if, at the end of that first call, Marcus had said, "When should we talk next? Does Tuesday at 10 work?" And the prospect had said yes, and both of them had put it on their calendars before hanging up.

Tuesday, Marcus doesn't send a follow-up email hoping for a reply. He shows up to a scheduled call. The conversation continues. The deal stays alive.

That's the difference between chasing and controlling. The next conversation agreed to in the room is worth ten follow-ups begged for after the room.

Study after study on deal velocity puts the same finding in front of us: deals with a clear next step move faster and close at higher rates. The reason is simple. A booked next conversation isn't just logistics. It's a signal. It tells both sides that this deal is real. It creates an anchor. The prospect has a date in their mind, a micro-commitment to the process.

And you have a clean call-back that nobody has to manufacture from scratch.

When you leave without booking the next step, you're handing control of the timeline to the prospect's calendar, their team, their inbox, their boss, and everything else competing for their attention. When you leave with a booked next step, you've kept one foot in the room even after you walked out of it.

This is the closest thing to a magic trick that exists in follow-up. Not because it's clever or manipulative. Because it's structural. The fifth conversation you're working toward becomes a lot more reachable when conversations two, three, and four are already on the calendar before you leave the first one.

The Anatomy of a Booked Next Step

The ideal booked next step has three parts. Not one, not two. Three. When a full booking isn't possible, use the downgrade ladder to secure the strongest available anchor.

A date. Specific. Not "sometime next week." Tuesday, March 4th at 10 a.m. The moment it gets a date, it gets a slot in both calendars. Slots are real. "Next week" is vapor.

A reason. What's happening between now and then? What will you know that you don't know now? What are you each going to prepare, confirm, or find out? If there's no reason to talk, there's no reason to show up. Give the next conversation a job.

What each side brings. This is the part most sellers skip, and it's the part that makes the next conversation feel like a continuation instead of a cold restart. "I'll bring the revised proposal with the two options we discussed. You'll have had a chance to talk to your operations lead. We'll start there."

Now you're not following up, you're reconvening. The dynamic is completely different.

Here's what that sounds like in practice. Weak close: "I'll follow up next week." Strong close: "Thursday at 2, you'll have had the board meeting, and I'll bring the updated pricing breakdown. Does that work?"

The strong version takes about ten extra seconds to say. Those ten seconds decide whether the next conversation happens or whether it slowly dies in your follow-up queue.

One more thing about the reason: it should connect to something they told you they'd know by then. "You said the budget decision gets made at the Thursday meeting. Can we schedule Friday morning, once you have the answer?" Now the next conversation has a natural gravity pulling it forward. They said Thursday was the decision point. You're coming back Friday. That's not pushy. That's organized.

Train yourself to listen for those future-pointing moments in every conversation. "We're waiting on the board." "I need to loop in my partner." "The pilot ends next month." Each one of those is a built-in reason for the next conversation. Catch it. Name it. Book it before you hang up.

Handling "I'll Call You"

You've heard it. You may have said it yourself to get off a call you didn't want to extend. "I'll reach out. I'll call you. I'll be in touch."

It means almost nothing. Prospects who say "I'll call you" are not lying, exactly. They mean it in the moment. But meaning it and doing it are two very different things. Their day will happen, your deal will drift, and the call will never come.

Your job is to gracefully not accept that answer.

This doesn't mean you push back, argue, or refuse to end the conversation. It means you ask one more question before you agree to wait.

"That works. Is there a day that's better for you to reconnect? I want to make sure I catch you when you have time, not just fire into your voicemail."

Most people will give you a day. And then you say, "Tuesday works. Morning or afternoon?" And you have half a booking.

The goal is a calendar invitation. Not a promise, not an agreement, not a "for sure, I'll be around." An actual calendar event sitting in both your inboxes, with a subject line that makes it real.

A calendar invitation does something a verbal commitment doesn't. It makes saying no a deliberate choice. To skip a scheduled call, they have to actively blow through it or cancel it. That's friction in your favor. A verbal "I'll call you" requires no action to break. They just don't call. Done.

When you can, send the invite while you're still on the call. "Let me shoot you a calendar invite right now so neither of us forgets." Most people will say yes. Some will say "I'll accept it when I'm back at my desk." That's fine. The invite is in their inbox either way.

The questions that get you there without pressure are simple. "What day works best?" is less loaded than "Can we schedule a call?" One feels like a search for a time, the other feels like a commitment being asked for. Let them find the day. You'll nail down the time.

And if they resist scheduling entirely? You don't argue. You move to the next move.

The Downgrade Ladder

Sometimes they won't book a specific time. That's okay. Your job isn't to force a booking, it's to leave with the best version of a next step that the moment allows.

The downgrade ladder is the sequence you move through when the ideal answer, a specific date and time, isn't available yet. The real requirement is simple: find the stall's actual trigger and record the return date.

Start with a specific date. "Does Tuesday at 2 work?" Try this first. It's the best outcome.

If they can't do a specific time right now, try a window. "What about the first week of March? I'll reach out Monday morning and we can pick a time from there." Now you have an anchor week. You're not following up blindly. You're showing up in a range they agreed to.

If even a window is too much to commit to, tie the next conversation to an event. "When does the funding close?" "When does your lease renewal come up?" "When does the new system go live?" "Why don't I reach out the day after that happens, once the dust settles a bit?" Their trigger becomes your calendar event.

Never leave with nothing. This is the rule. Even if all you get is "I'll know more in about a month," that's still something. "Great. I'll reach out in four weeks. Does the first week of April work as a target?" You've turned vague timing into a loose anchor.

A loose anchor is better than nothing. Nothing means you're starting over from scratch, guessing when to call, hoping they pick up, wondering if you're too early or too late.

Moving down the ladder doesn't feel like losing. It feels like staying connected to reality. You know your deal is in a slow moment, and you're keeping a thread tied to it instead of cutting the line and hoping they find you later.

Practice the ladder in order every time. Work down only if you have to. Most of the time, you won't have to. Most people will book a call if you ask the right way at the right moment, before the energy drains out of the conversation.

That timing matters. The close of a good conversation is the highest-leverage moment to book the next one. The energy is up, the trust is fresh, and they're still thinking about you. Ask before the warmth fades. Ask while you're both still in it.

Train It Everywhere

Here's what most sellers do with a habit like this. They read about it. They think it sounds smart. They use it once or twice the next day and it feels a little awkward because they haven't built the reflex yet. A week later they're back to "I'll follow up" and the habit is gone.

That's not a knowledge problem. That's a training problem.

The way you build this reflex is the same way you'd build any physical skill. You train it repeatedly until it's automatic. You don't wait for the hard situation. You train it in the easy situations first.

For the next week, end every single business conversation by booking the next one. Not just sales calls. Every business conversation. The internal meeting. The call with your vendor. The check-in with a colleague. When it ends, ask: "When should we connect next?"

You'll feel a little odd at first. That's exactly what you want. Odd means you're working a muscle you haven't used this way before. The soreness is the point.

By conversation ten, you'll feel the reflex forming. By conversation twenty, it won't feel like a technique at all. It'll feel like the obvious way to end a conversation. Because it is.

The reason to train it in easy conversations is that easy conversations have low stakes. You can flub the timing, stumble on the wording, forget to send the invite, and none of it costs you a deal. But you still get the rep. And the reps stack.

When you train any physical skill, you don't start with the competition. You drill it in the gym first. A gymnast doesn't learn a new dismount by attempting it in front of judges. She trains it in practice, over and over, until the body knows the movement without being told. Then she takes it to the arena.

You don't rise to the occasion. You fall back on how you've trained.

If you've never practiced booking the next conversation under low-stakes conditions, the high-stakes conversation is a terrible place to try it for the first time. Train it now, in every conversation, so that when the big deal is wrapping up and you feel the pull to say "I'll follow up," your trained reflex steps in and asks the question anyway.

Here's something worth noticing: this habit helps you on the deals that are going well, too. Maybe especially on those.

When a conversation goes great, the temptation is to coast. The vibe was good, they're interested, it'll be fine. But deals don't die only when things go badly. They die when you let momentum stop. Momentum is easiest to keep when you never let it stop.

The deals that go sideways after a strong first call aren't usually killed by something the prospect did. They drift. The seller got comfortable. Assumed it was locked. Waited a little too long. And in that gap, something else entered the picture. A competitor called. An internal priority shifted. The window closed.

Book the next conversation even when things are going great. Especially when things are going great. Don't let a strong conversation become the high-water mark. Make it the first good step in a sequence that ends in a closed deal.

Build the Habit Into Your Closing Sequence

Think of the final two minutes of every sales conversation as a distinct phase. Like the dismount at the end of a gymnastics routine. You can't improvise the landing. You train it until it's a sequence, and you run the sequence every time.

The last two minutes have a job: confirm understanding, establish the next step, put it on the calendar.

Confirm understanding sounds like: "So where we are is, you're interested and the main question is whether the timeline works for Q2. Does that match where you're at?"

Establish the next step sounds like: "When does it make sense to pick this back up? What would you know by then that you don't know today?"

Put it on the calendar sounds like: "Let me send you an invite. What email do you want it to go to?"

Three moves. Same order every time. You can adapt the language to fit your style, your market, your personality. What you can't adapt is skipping a move. The sequence holds.

When all three moves land, you're done. When one gets interrupted or resisted, you've got the downgrade ladder to fall back on. Either way, you know your sequence, you know your fallback, and you're not improvising in the most important thirty seconds of the call.

Picture a rep, call her Kira. She used to end calls with "I'll be in touch." She tracked her follow-up rate and found that fewer than a third of her "I'll be in touch" deals made it to a second conversation within two weeks. Some took a month. Some never happened.

She started running the three-move close on every call. Inside a month, her second-conversation rate had climbed significantly. The deals weren't better. The prospects weren't different. The only thing that changed was what she said in the last two minutes.

The close of the conversation is the bridge to the fifth conversation. Build that bridge before you leave the room.

Your Rep

The Drill. For one week, end every single business conversation by booking the next one. This means sales calls, internal check-ins, vendor calls, client updates. Every conversation gets a next step before it closes. Track how many times you succeed. Write the number down at the end of each day. By day seven, you'll know your real booking rate.

The Questions.

"When should we talk next?"

"What will you know by then that you don't know now?"

"Does Thursday at 2 work, or is Friday morning better?"

"Let me send you a calendar invite right now. What email should I use?"

"When does the funding close? Why don't I reach out the day after?"

Train It. The 90-day version of this drill is in The Fifth Conversation Workbook, at ConvoControl.com/fifthconversation.

Chapter Seven

The Follow-Up Ladder

How often should you follow up? Wrong question. The right one: what rung is this deal on?

Most sellers think about follow-up frequency as a fixed setting. Like there's one right answer that applies to every deal, every person, every stage of the conversation. There isn't. A deal that's two days from a signed contract and a deal where someone said "maybe next year" are not the same deal. They don't get the same touch. They don't get the same rhythm. Treating them identically is how you over-contact the people who are almost ready and under-contact the people you've quietly given up on.

The Follow-Up Ladder fixes that. It's a simple framework: every open deal in your pipeline lives on one rung of a four-level ladder, and each rung has its own natural rhythm. You don't have to guess. You don't have to feel it out. You look at the deal, you put it on the right rung, and the rung tells you what to do next.

Here's what the ladder looks like.

The Ladder Concept

Four rungs. Four rhythms.

Hot. The deal is in motion. A decision is coming. They've asked for a proposal, they're talking to their partner, they're circling back with the board at the end of the week. Something real is happening on their side. Hot deals get a touch every 48 to 72 hours. Not a hounding message, not the same question twice, but a relevant, short, value-forward check-in on the cadence that matches where they actually are. When someone is this close to moving, silence from your side is dangerous. They can talk themselves out of it. They can get distracted. They can hear from a competitor. You stay present.

Warm. They're interested. They asked thoughtful questions in the first conversation, they said they'd bring it to their team, there's real intent here but the clock is slower. No imminent decision date, no urgent problem on fire. Warm deals get one touch per week. Enough to stay in their awareness, not so much that you become the rep who just won't let it go. Weekly contact gives them room to breathe while keeping you as the obvious next call when something shifts.

Stalled. You've got a logged "no for now." Budget's frozen, they're mid-project on something else, they told you to come back in a few months. You know the trigger, you know the approximate date, and you're waiting for the right moment to re-open. Stalled deals get a touch every two to three weeks. Often, this touch is a piece of value, something relevant to their world, with a light question attached. You're keeping the relationship warm without rushing a timeline that isn't yours to set.

Long game. Genuine "not now." Could be six months away, could be a year. There's no current urgency on their side and no specific trigger you're waiting on. Long-game deals get one touch per quarter. Once every three months. That might feel like too little, but it isn't. It's exactly enough to stay real without becoming noise.

Now here's the skill that separates trained follow-up from amateur follow-up: moving deals down the ladder on purpose. When a hot deal cools down, most sellers panic or disappear. The right move is to step them deliberately from hot to warm, tell them you're doing it, and keep the rhythm. Something like: "Sounds like the timing's shifted a bit on your end. I'll check back in a week rather than tomorrow. Does that work?" You've acknowledged the new pace, you've kept the conversation open, and you've held your place in the deal without pressure.

The ladder fails when you vanish.

The Vanish Is the Cardinal Sin

Picture a rep, call him Marcus. He finds a prospect, has a great first call, sends a proposal, texts twice that week, calls on Friday. Then nothing. Silence. Two weeks go by. A month. The deal doesn't close, so it drifts to the bottom of his CRM and Marcus tells himself the prospect just wasn't ready.

What the prospect experienced was different. They saw someone who was very interested, then completely gone. And when you go from high-touch to zero touch with no explanation, the prospect learns something about you. They learn you were chasing the commission, not committed to them. The interest was real as long as the deal looked likely. The moment it got complicated, you evaporated.

Ghosting from the seller side is different from ghosting from the prospect side. When a prospect goes quiet, there's usually a reason and usually a move you can make (chapters 13 and 14 cover that in full).

When a seller goes quiet, there's never a good reason. You decided to stop. That's it.

The vanish is the most common mistake in follow-up, and it's the hardest one to see from inside it. You're not thinking "I'm giving up." You're thinking "I'll get back to this when there's something new to say." But days turn into weeks and the deal cools from the outside while it feels like it's just sitting there waiting.

The fix is the downward movement. When a deal slows, move it down a rung. Hot to warm. Warm to stalled. Move it deliberately, tell the prospect if appropriate, and keep one hand on the deal. A deal on the long-game rung is still in your pipeline. A deal you vanished from is in someone else's.

Climb down a rung. Keep the rhythm. Never disappear.

Timing Windows That Actually Work

Okay, so you know what rung a deal is on. You know your cadence. But when do you actually make the call? When do you send the message?

This matters more than most people acknowledge. Send the right thing at the wrong time and it gets missed or ignored.

For business owners and entrepreneurs: your window is early morning or after close. We're talking before 8am or after 5pm. Business owners are usually knee-deep in their operation during the work day. Mid-rush is the worst possible time to reach someone who's running a shop, managing a crew, or putting out the day's fires. But before the doors open? Before the customers show up? Before their team needs them? That's quiet time. They're often doing email, doing planning, getting ahead. Same with after hours. A short, relevant message landing at 6:45am or 6:30pm has a much better chance than the same message at 11am.

For corporate buyers and managers: mid-week, mid-morning. Tuesday through Wednesday, with Wednesday being the highest, is the optimal outreach window for corporate buyers and manager s.[1] Monday morning is a disaster, people are catching up, triaging the inbox, getting oriented for the week. By Monday afternoon they're buried. Friday afternoon they're already mentally out the door, counting down to the weekend. Wednesday at 10am, though? They're in the groove. The week is underway, the urgent fires are handled, and they have the headspace to engage with something new.

For consumers: evenings and weekends. If you're selling B2C and your buyer is a regular person with a regular job, they're not checking personal messages at 2pm on a Tuesday. They're working. Your window is weekday evenings, Saturday morning, or early Sunday before the day fills up.

These are general patterns, not laws of physics. You'll meet the corporate buyer who answers texts at 7am and the business owner who's unreachable before 10. Pay attention to when each specific person actually responds to you, because that pattern is your real window. But when you have no data yet, these defaults give you a starting point that's much better than guessing.

One more timing rule that almost everyone ignores: match your send time to your message type. A text goes out when they're likely reading texts. An email with detail in it goes out when they're likely sitting at a desk. A LinkedIn message goes out during business hours when they're probably checked in to their professional world. Channel timing and message timing should move together.

B2B vs. B2C Rhythms

The ladder rungs are universal. The rhythm layered on top of them is not. Your prospect's world shapes when your touches land and what they need to say.

B2B runs on the work calendar. Budget cycles, fiscal years, quarters, board meetings, headcount decisions. If your prospect's budget opens in January, it doesn't matter how warm you keep the relationship in October. The deal can't move until January. What you can do is stay in contact so you're first in line when January arrives, but you're not forcing a Q4 decision on someone whose hands are tied until Q1.

Know the calendar rhythms in your market. When does budget typically get approved? When do new fiscal years start? When are the big planning cycles that mean nobody makes new vendor decisions for six weeks? These aren't obstacles. They're information. If you know their fiscal year ends in June, a conversation in March about the following budget cycle is well-timed. The same conversation in November, when the budget is already locked, is just friction.

B2C runs on life rhythms. Paydays. Seasons. Life events. Tax return season. The start of a new school year. The week after a birthday. The moment someone's lease is up or their kid heads to college. If you sell something that's relevant to those life moments, your cadence should account for them. A touch right after a payday often lands differently than the same touch mid-month when the account is thin. This isn't manipulation. It's timing. You're meeting people where they are, not forcing them into a timeline that serves only you.

One practical tip that doesn't get said enough: ask. In your first or second conversation, ask about their decision calendar directly. Something like: "Is there a better time of year for conversations like this, or does timing not really matter for you?" That one question can tell you everything you need to know about how to pace the next six months. They'll tell you if Q2 is always slammed, or if December is actually when they're planning ahead, or if they make these decisions on their own schedule regardless of the calendar. Write it down. Use it .

The common thread in B2B and B2C is this: the cadence serves them, not you. Your urgency is not their urgency. If you show up with the right rhythm at the right times, you're a resource. If you show up constantly at the wrong times, you're noise they learn to filter.

How Many Touches Before You Move On?

Before we get to building the system, there's a question that comes up every time this topic surfaces: how many touches do I give a deal before I move it to the long game or walk away?

The key word is meaningful. A touch is a message that carries some value, a relevant insight, a question tied to their situation, a piece of proof, a re-open of something they mentioned. Sending the same "just wanted to check in" message eight times is not eight touches. It's one bad touch, repeated.

When you've sent a meaningful series of touches with no response and no engagement, that's your signal to make one honest move, the closing-the-file question (chapter 13 covers this fully), and then move the deal to the long-game rung. Don't delete it. Don't mark it lost. Move it down. Quarterly touches, no pressure, keep building the relationship at a lower cadence. The fifth conversation sometimes happens a year after the first. Plenty of deals that went completely cold in month three close in month nine when the prospect's situation changes and they remember the rep who never stopped showing up.

Patience is not weakness. It's strategy.

Build It Into the Calendar

Here's where most people lose the game. They read about the ladder, they agree with the logic, they maybe even decide which rung their top deals sit on. Then Monday comes, the inbox fires up, and follow-up becomes reactive instead of scheduled. They touch the deals that happen to come to mind. They forget the ones that have gone quiet. The system they almost built dissolves into habit.

The fix is simple and most people skip it because it feels too basic: every touch gets scheduled the moment the last one finishes.

You send a follow-up on a hot deal. Right then, before you do anything else, you create the calendar reminder or the CRM task for the next touch. Forty-eight hours from now. Done. You sent a warm-deal message. Schedule next week's touch. Now. You moved a deal from warm to stalled. Add a two-to-three week task. You just had a conversation that ended with "call me in Q3." Put the Q3 date in your calendar immediately, with the re-open question already written in the task notes.

If it doesn't get scheduled in the moment, it probably doesn't get scheduled at all. Your future self will be just as busy as your current self. Don't outsource the memory to intention. Put it on the calendar while the conversation is still fresh.

This also creates something useful: a visual. When your calendar has your follow-up touches blocked out across the next 30 days for your top deals, you can see your pipeline activity at a glance. You can see where you've been consistent and where there are gaps. You can see which deals haven't had a scheduled touch in three weeks, which is the early warning sign for a deal you're about to vanish from.

The system doesn't require fancy software. It requires a reflex. Schedule the next touch before you close the window on the last one.

That's it. Repeat it every day. Watch what happens to your pipeline in 60 days.

One practical structure that works well: every Friday, spend ten minutes looking at next week's scheduled touches. Do you have coverage on your hot deals? Are the warm ones accounted for? Any stalled deals that have slipped past their touch date? That ten-minute check is the difference between a pipeline you're managing and a pipeline that's managing you.

The person who controls the conversation controls the outcome, and controlling the follow-up cadence is how you stay in control of conversations that aren't happening in real time.

Your Rep

The Drill. Take your top five open deals right now. For each one, write down the rung it belongs on: hot, warm, stalled, or long game. Based on that rung, figure out when the next touch should happen. Then schedule every single touch for those five deals across the next 30 days. Don't just think about it. Get it on the calendar before you close this chapter.

The Questions.

"What rung is this deal on today?"

"When is this specific person actually reachable, based on their world, not mine?"

"When did I last touch this deal, and when is the next one scheduled?"

Train It. The complete Follow-Up Ladder template, with every rung and rhythm from this chapter, is free at ConvoControl.com/fifthconversation. Print it, fill it in, put it on the wall.

Chapter Eight

Educational, Not Pushy

Do you want to be pushy, or do you want to be educational? You're going to be one of them.

There's no neutral option here. When a deal slows down and you reach back out, you are either adding something or you're not. You're either giving them a reason to open the next message or you're training them to ignore you. The choice between those two paths is the choice this chapter is about.

Most sellers make the wrong one by default, because nobody taught them there was another option.

The Fork

A deal goes quiet. You haven't heard from them in a week. Your instinct tells you to do something, so you do what feels like action. You send a follow-up. Maybe it's a nudge. Maybe it's a reminder that the price goes up next month. Maybe it's a third email asking if they've had a chance to look things over. You're moving, and moving feels like progress.

It isn't.

When you push, you spend trust. Every nudge, every pressure-touch, every manufactured deadline withdraws from the account you built during the first conversation. The prospect feels it even if they can't name it. Something shifts from "this person might actually help me" to "this person really wants to close me." And once that shift happens, getting them back is harder than getting the original meeting.

The trained move is different. When a deal slows, you teach.

Teaching means you send something useful. A relevant article about a problem they mentioned. A short summary of what you've seen work for similar situations. A question that helps them think through where they are. You show up not as a vendor chasing a PO but as someone who knows their space and is genuinely interested in their situation.

The distinction matters because of what it does to the relationship over time. Pushing keeps the focus on your timeline. Teaching keeps the focus on their problem. And buyers do business with the people focused on their problem.

Picture a rep, call her Priya. She's been in follow-up mode for six weeks on a mid-market deal that stalled after a great second call. Her instinct was to check in every week, remind them of the ROI numbers they'd discussed, and mention twice that the implementation slots were filling up. She got one polite reply and then silence.

She switched her approach. Instead of checking in, she started sending short, specific notes about things directly connected to what they'd discussed: a relevant shift happening in their industry, a question about a challenge the contact had mentioned almost offhand in their second call. No pitch. No mention of the deal. Just useful things, wrapped in a question.

On the fourth touch of this kind, the reply came back. "Sorry for going dark. Things have been crazy. This is actually really timely."

The deal didn't come back because she pushed harder. It came back because she stayed useful.

The Four Value Touches and the Send Test

Every follow-up touch you send should deliver at least one thing from this list. If it delivers none of them, it doesn't go out.

A relevant insight. Something useful about their world, their industry, or their specific situation. It doesn't have to be long. One paragraph, one link, one observation. The test: could you send this to anyone, or is it clearly for them? Generic insights don't land. Specific ones do. Something like a shift in their industry that affects the problem they're trying to solve.

A piece of proof. A result someone like them got. A before-and-after story from your world. A real number from a comparable situation. Just one example of the value you can bring.

A useful introduction. Someone they should know. A connection you can make that serves them whether or not they ever buy from you. This one is underused and wildly effective. When you introduce two people who genuinely benefit from knowing each other, you become the person who does that. That's a hard reputation to compete with.

A question that advances their thinking. Not a sales question. Not "where are we on timing?" A question about their situation that makes them stop and actually think. "You mentioned the team was stretched thin. Has that changed going into Q4?" "What's the pressure looking like now that the quarter's closing?" These questions position you as someone paying attention to their world, not just to your pipeline.

One touch, one value. That's the rule.

And before anything goes out, there's a test. One question. "Would they thank me for this?" Not "would this help me?" Not "does this move the deal forward?" Would they, the person you're sending it to, look at this message and feel like their day got a little better because it arrived?

If yes, send it.

If no, or if you're not sure, don't. Go back to the value bank (more on that in a moment) and find something that passes the test.

The send test sounds simple because it is. But it's also a real filter that most sellers never apply. It forces you to think about your follow-up from their side of the inbox, not yours. That shift alone separates a lot of dead deals from live ones.

Staying Relevant in the Noise

Your prospect's inbox is not a quiet place. They're getting dozens, sometimes hundreds of messages every day, from vendors who all sound roughly the same. Most of those messages are about the sender. Their product. Their availability. Their pricing. Their value proposition, usually listed in bullet points.

Yours doesn't have to sound like that.

When someone opens your message and it's useful, actually useful, to their real situation, it lands differently. They notice it. Maybe they don't reply right away. Maybe they save it. But they've registered that you're the one sending things worth reading. That's a different relationship than the vendor they're mentally ignoring.

Attention isn't won by frequency. You can touch someone every single day and get no reply if everything you send is noise. You can touch them once a week with something genuinely useful and become the person they look forward to hearing from. One is a numbers game. The other is a quality game. And quality is the one that scales, because trust compounds.

There's another layer here that most sellers miss. You are not just competing against other sellers in your space. You're competing against everything in their day. The internal fires. The meetings that shouldn't be meetings. The message from the person three levels above them that just landed and moved everything else down the list. In that environment, a message that's clearly useful is the message that gets through. A message that's clearly a nudge is the message that gets deleted later, when they batch-clear their inbox on a Friday.

So the question becomes: in an inbox full of noise, how do you consistently be the signal?

You do it by knowing their world well enough to say something true and useful about it. You do it by paying attention in every conversation so you have material to draw from. You do it by treating every follow-up touch as a chance to actually be helpful, not just as a step in a sequence.

That's not a script. It's a posture.

Build the Value Bank

The reason most sellers resort to check-ins and nudges isn't laziness. They sit down to write the follow-up and there's nothing there. A blank screen, a stalled deal, and no idea what to say that isn't "just wanted to follow up."

The value bank solves that problem before it starts.

A value bank is a simple collection of useful things you've already gathered, organized so you can find them when you need them. You build it once, add to it regularly, and pull from it every time you need a touch. Here's what goes in it.

Ten market insights. These are things happening in your prospect's world that they probably care about. Shifts in their industry. Changes in regulation or technology that affect how they work. Patterns you see across the conversations you're having. You don't need to be a journalist to build this list. You need to read what's happening in your space and save the pieces that make you think "my clients would want to know this."

Five proof pieces. Real results, or as close to real as you can document.

A folder of share-worthy content. Articles, short videos, research pieces, opinion pieces from credible voices in their space. Save things that are actually useful, not things that happen to mention your product. The test: would you send this to a friend who worked in that industry and not feel embarrassed?

A list of introductions you can make. Five to ten people in your network who serve similar clients in a non-competing way. When the right connection comes up, you can offer it without scrambling to think of someone. "I know someone who works specifically on this" is a different kind of follow-up than any email you could write.

A set of thinking questions. Five to ten open questions that advance the prospect's thinking about their own situation. Not sales questions. Questions that, if someone asked them in a real conversation, would make you feel like they genuinely understood what you were dealing with. Save these so you're never starting from scratch.

One hour to build the core of this bank. Thirty minutes a week to keep it current. That's the whole maintenance cost.

Once you have it, the blank screen problem disappears. You open the bank, pick the piece that fits this person and this moment, wrap it in a question, and send it. The problem of "I don't know what to say" stops being a problem because you've already done the preparation.

This is the same logic that applies to any performance under pressure. You don't rise to the occasion. You fall back on how you've trained. The value bank is training. It's the prep work that lets you show up consistently, even on the days when you're busy and the pipeline feels like a grind.

The Repositioning Effect

Here's something that happens with educational follow-up that most sellers don't anticipate.

After three educational touches, the relationship changes.

You started the deal as a vendor. Someone who showed up with a product and a pitch and a price. That's the role the prospect put you in during the first conversation. It's where most sellers stay, because they keep showing up with things that remind the prospect that's what they are.

When you show up with insight, proof, introductions, and thinking questions instead, the perception shifts. You become something different. Not a vendor chasing a sale. An advisor who actually knows their world, cares about their situation, and keeps showing up with useful things regardless of whether the deal is moving.

That status change does something powerful. It makes you harder to ignore. Ignoring a vendor is easy. Ignoring an advisor who keeps being helpful feels different. It creates a kind of social weight that works in your favor. They start to feel like they'd be missing something if they let this relationship go.

This isn't manipulation. The prospect isn't tricked into anything. You're genuinely being useful. The repositioning is a side effect of actually doing the work, not a trick layered on top of it.

And when the timing is finally right, when the budget opens or the problem gets loud enough or the thing they were waiting on finally resolves, you're not a vendor they half-remember from a call three months ago. You're the person who's been in their corner. The choice isn't "should we buy from this company?" It's "when do we move forward with the person we've been talking to?"

That's a very different conversation to be in.

Picture a rep, call him Marcus. He had a deal that stalled after the first call and sat for four months with zero activity. He came back to it with three educational touches over six weeks. An industry trend piece with a question about how it was landing for them. A short proof story about a comparable situation, with "Is this similar to what you're dealing with?" at the end. A connection to someone in his network who solved an adjacent problem.

On the fourth touch, the prospect replied: "Honestly, we should just get this done. You've been more helpful in the last month than our current provider has been all year."

Marcus didn't outsell anyone. He out-taught them. He stayed in the conversation when everyone else left. That's the fifth conversation in action.

The Repositioning Effect in Practice

The repositioning doesn't happen from one good touch. It builds. And it builds faster than most sellers expect, because the bar is so low.

Your prospect is surrounded by vendors who never send anything useful. When you do, consistently, you don't have to be extraordinary.

You just have to be reliably good. One useful thing every week or two, over the course of a month or two, and you have built something no pitch can buy.

There's a discipline to it, though. It's easy to be educational when the deal feels hot. It's much harder when the deal has been quiet for six weeks and you've got other things demanding your attention. The sellers who understand that consistency is the point, not just the tactic, are the ones who get the calls that say "sorry for the delay, let's pick this back up."

The send test is what keeps the discipline honest. Every time you're tempted to send the check-in email because you haven't heard anything and you need to do something, you run the test. "Would they thank me for this?" If the answer is no, you go back to the bank. You find the thing that passes.

Sometimes the right move is to wait a few days until you have something worth sending. That's not inaction. That's discipline. The touch you don't send because it wasn't good enough is better than the touch you do send that trains the prospect to tune you out.

This is the chapter that feeds everything that comes next. Proof, which we cover in Chapter 9, is one category of value. Sounding human, which is Chapter 10, is how value lands. The questions in Chapter 12 are the delivery mechanism. All of it connects. But the foundation, the thing underneath all the tactics, is that you made a decision early in the deal to be educational.

Keep making that decision every time you reach out.

Your Rep

The Drill. This week, build the first version of your value bank. Pull ten insights about your market, five proof pieces, and a list of five introductions you could make. Then pick one item from the bank and send it to a stalled deal today, with a single question attached at the end. Don't mention the deal. Don't mention timing. Just send the thing and ask the question.

The Questions. These are the questions to send with your value-bank touches. Train with them, adapt them to your language and market, and find the ones that consistently get replies.

- "Saw this and thought of your situation. Does it match what you're seeing on your side?"

- "A company about your size just solved this a different way. Want the short version?"

- "Who on your team is feeling this problem the most right now?"

- "This reminded me of what you said about [specific thing they mentioned]. Is that still the piece that's hardest to solve?"

- "Would it be useful if I put together a short summary of how similar situations have played out? I can keep it to two or three paragraphs."

Train It. The 90-day version of this drill, including a structured value bank template and a weekly touch tracker, is in The Fifth Conversation Workbook, at ConvoControl.com/fifthconversation.

Chapter Nine

Proof Does the Talking

By the third conversation, they've heard everything you have to say about yourself. So who else is going to say it?

Think about where you actually are by touch three. You've made your case. You've answered their early questions. You sent the recap. You walked them through the offer, the process, the timeline, the fit. You said the right things and they nodded in the right places.

They heard you. They still haven't moved.

So the instinct kicks in to go again. Same message, different format. Another email, longer this time. New bullet points. A tighter explanation. More of you making the same argument you already made.

Here's the thing: the argument has been made. You're not facing a prospect who hasn't heard your case. You're facing one who has heard it and still hasn't committed. Saying it again, in different packaging, is the same touch. It just has a later date on it.

What actually breaks a stall at this stage is a different voice. And the only voice that's genuinely new by conversation three is someone who isn't you.

That's what proof does. It shows up after your own words have run their course. It hands the mic to someone who's already been exactly where your prospect is standing right now, and came out the other side.

Why Proof Is the Follow-Up Weapon

Most sellers think of proof as a pitch tool. The case study on slide nine. The testimonial on the website. The results page built into the proposal. You use it in the room to bolster your claims, and then you move on.

That's one use. But it's not where proof does its best work.

Proof is more powerful in follow-up than it ever is in the initial pitch. The reason has everything to do with where your prospect's head is at the two different stages.

In the pitch, they're in evaluation mode. They're listening for red flags, forming an impression, trying to figure out if you're credible. Proof lands, but it lands inside a skeptical filter. They're still deciding if they believe you.

By the third or fourth touch, that filter has shifted. They've already formed an opinion about you. They're past the credibility question. Now they're asking a different one: has anyone else actually done this? Will it work for a situation like mine? Am I going to look smart for saying yes, or am I taking on unnecessary risk?

That's a completely different question. And the only thing that truly answers it is someone who came in with the same doubt and made it to the other side.

You cannot be your own witness. You can describe the result from the outside, but you didn't need the solution yourself. Your prospect knows that. They're not looking for your testimony about your own product. They're looking for someone they can relate to who's already made the decision they're being asked to make.

Study after study on purchase behavior finds social proof consistently near the top of what breaks a buying stall. When people are uncertain, they look at what others like them did. This is true for small decisions and large ones. It's true in B2B and B2C. The prospect who's been sitting on your proposal for three weeks may not be unconvinced. They may just be looking for someone to go first.

Give them that person.

There's a reason this chapter sits here, right after the educational touches in Chapter 8 and the value bank you've been building. You've been showing up with useful information. That repositioning effect has been working. You're starting to feel less like a vendor and more like an advisor.

The proof touch completes that shift. An advisor doesn't just share knowledge. An advisor brings evidence. When you send proof at this stage of the follow-up sequence, you're not pitching again. You're saying: here's someone who was where you are, here's what they chose, here's what changed. The conversation becomes about them, not about you.

That's the lever. And it's one your competitors probably aren't pulling, because they're still busy resending the deck.

Here's what makes this especially valuable in the fifth conversation context. Most sellers are long gone by touch four. They gave up after one or two attempts, convinced the deal was dead. You're still there. And when you show up at touch four with a proof piece that mirrors your prospect's exact situation, you're not just delivering new information. You're demonstrating a kind of staying power that the proof piece itself reinforces. If other customers trusted you enough to get results, and you've stayed in this conversation long enough to say so, that combination signals something.

It signals you're the real thing.

The Anatomy of Proof That Works

There's a clear line between proof that stops people and proof that gets scrolled past. The line is specificity.

"Our clients love us" lives on the wrong side of that line. So does "results-driven" and "trusted by businesses nationwide" and every other phrase that costs nothing to type and says nothing that matters. These are adjectives pretending to be evidence. They create no picture. They answer no question. They give your prospect nothing to hold onto.

Real proof has texture. It has detail. It sounds like a real situation because it is one.

Picture a rep, call her Dana. Dana sells consulting services to small manufacturing companies. She's two conversations in with a prospect, a family-run operation that had heard good things about her but was hesitant to commit. The issue wasn't price. It was risk. They'd worked with a vendor before who promised results and delivered chaos.

Dana sent a proof touch. She described a company similar in size, in a related industry, that had started with the same concern. That company decided to run a limited pilot before committing fully. The pilot went well. They expanded. A few months later, their throughput had improved enough that they brought on additional staff from the savings the change had created.

One email. One story. One question at the end: "Would a pilot approach like that make sense as a starting point for you?"

The prospect replied that afternoon.

Look at the anatomy of what Dana sent. A named person. A hard number. A situation that resembles theirs. And one connecting question as the delivery. That's the formula. Every time.

Three elements, always together: a named person, a hard number, a situation that resembles theirs. The connecting question is how you hand it over, not a fourth element. It's the delivery.

The situation needs to be close enough to theirs to feel relatable. Same size, same industry if you have it, same type of problem. If your prospect is a five-person team worried about adoption, don't lead with a story about a Fortune 500 rollout. That story isn't a mirror. It's a painting in a museum. Impressive but irrelevant.

The result needs to be concrete. "Things improved significantly" doesn't move people. "They went from losing three deals a month to follow-up gaps to recapturing two of them in the first six weeks" moves people. Specifics persuade. Adjectives evaporate. Give them a number, a timeline, a before and after they can hold in their hand.

The question needs to tie the story directly back to their situation. Not "hope this helps" or "let me know what you think." Those are conversation enders. A question is a conversation opener. "Does this look anything like where you are right now?" or "Is the timing concern still the main thing, or has something else moved up?" Those questions pull the story through to their specific decision.

Miss one element and the proof loses its punch. The situation without the result is just a vague anecdote. The result without the situation is a claim with no context. The result and situation without the question are a case study with no call to action.

One more note on relevance. Your biggest, most dramatic case study might not be your best proof touch for a given prospect. The story that looks most like their world, even if the result was modest, will outperform a blockbuster win that feels distant from what they're dealing with. Find the mirror, not the trophy.

The Proof Touch

Now let's talk delivery. How do you actually turn a proof piece into a follow-up touch that gets opened, read, and replied to?

The structure is this: one proof piece, one connecting question. Nothing else.

Not a long email with the case study buried in paragraph three. Not a newsletter with five sections and a link at the bottom. One short story, one question. That's the whole touch.

Here's what the format looks like in practice. Say you're reaching out to a prospect who's been quiet for three weeks after asking for the proposal. You know from your conversation that their hesitation is about adoption. Their team is already stretched thin and they're worried about adding something new that creates more work instead of less. Here's a proof touch for that situation:

"Thought of you today. A team in a similar spot came in with the same adoption concern. We started them smaller than they planned, focused only on the piece that was causing the most friction. Within the first month, two of the skeptics on their team had become advocates. Is the adoption question still the main thing, or has something else moved up for you?"

Short. Specific. Ends with a question that locates where they actually are.

The question does two things simultaneously. It makes replying easy, because it's asking something concrete and answerable. And it surfaces new information. If their concern has shifted from adoption to budget, you want to know that. The question opens the door to the real conversation that needs to happen.

The proof touch works best in the middle stretch of a follow-up sequence. Touch three, four, or five. Early enough that the deal still has momentum you can tap. Late enough that you've fully made your own case and a new voice is genuinely new information rather than just more of the same.

You can deliver this touch across channels. Email gives you room for the two or three sentence setup. A text version works if you've earned that permission, and you keep it to one sentence plus the question. A phone call version works well too: "I wanted to share something quick before we hang up" followed by the story out loud, then the question. The format flexes. The structure stays the same.

Resist the urge to stack proof pieces. Sending two case studies, a review link, and a results page all in one message doesn't multiply the impact. It dilutes it. One piece competes with nothing. Five pieces compete with each other, and all five lose. Keep it to one. Make it count. End with a question.

And a timing note: once you've sent a proof touch, give the prospect a day or two before following up again. The proof touch does its work after the message is read, sometimes a few hours later when they're thinking about the decision again. You don't need to stack another touch on top of it immediately. Let it breathe.

The Silent Follow-Up and Borrowed Trust

Here's something most sellers don't think about enough.

In between every conversation you have with a prospect, they're checking you out.

Not formally. Just the low-key research anyone does when they're considering working with someone. They search your name. They look at your LinkedIn. They scan for reviews. They check your website or your social presence. They're trying to verify, without asking you directly, that you're the real thing.

This happens in the gaps between your touches. While you're planning your next move, they're making their own assessment. And what they find, or don't find, is either working for you or quietly working against you.

Call it the silent follow-up. Your online trail is in the deal whether you put it there intentionally or not.

Here's what the wrong version looks like. A prospect just had a strong first conversation with a seller. Good energy, good questions, genuinely interested but not ready to commit. That night, they search the seller's name. The LinkedIn profile hasn't been updated in over a year. The recommendations section is sparse. The company page has a couple of posts from two years back and nothing recent. They look for reviews and find a few old ones that are vague. No recent content, no visible activity, no sign that this person is busy and thriving.

Nothing about that experience says: this is someone who's doing well. This is someone active in their market. This is the real thing.

Does the prospect walk away immediately? Probably not. But a seed of doubt gets planted. And in a competitive deal, doubt compounds.

Now flip it. Same prospect, same conversation. That night they search and find an active profile with a clear bio and specific positioning. A handful of recommendations that read like they came from real people dealing with real situations. Some content, even just a few thoughtful posts, that signals the seller knows their market and participates in it. A review or two that confirms what the seller said in conversation.

The seller didn't do anything different in that conversation. The trail did the work.

This is your silent follow-up either working for you or against you right now. Audit it. Not what you intend to have online, what actually exists today when someone searches you. Go look. It takes five minutes and the information matters more than most sellers realize.

Building the trail doesn't have to be complicated. A current profile. A handful of genuine recommendations from people in relevant situations. Some evidence that you're active and engaged in your market. That's enough to back up the case you're making in your conversations.

Now for the second piece of this section.

There's a form of proof that most sellers underuse, and it might be the most powerful one in the toolkit.

The mutual connection.

When someone your prospect already knows and trusts says a single genuine word on your behalf, the dynamic changes completely. The trust transfers. It arrives pre-loaded, without needing a case study or a results page or an explanation.

A peer saying "you should talk to this person, she helped us work through the exact same thing" carries more weight than any email you could write, no matter how well crafted that email is. Human beings have been trusting referrals from people they know for as long as there have been transactions. The dynamic doesn't change because the transaction happens over Zoom now.

So when you're at touch four on a stalled deal and you've already made your case, ask one question before planning your next move. Is there anyone in your network who knows this prospect? Someone who could make a brief, genuine introduction or say a single word?

If the answer is yes and you haven't used that card, use it now.

The ask to a mutual contact doesn't need to be complicated. "Hey, I've been working with someone in your network on a challenge I think I can help them solve. Would you be open to a quick note of introduction?" Most people will say yes if the ask is small and genuinely in their friend's interest.

A line from someone they already trust can carry more weight than another email from you. That's the leverage. Use it.

Collecting Proof Deliberately

Everything in this chapter only works if you have proof to use when you need it.

That sounds obvious. But most sellers don't have a proof collection habit. They have proof collection intentions. They know they should be gathering testimonials and capturing results. They plan to build a proper system. They'll get to it after this quarter.

Then they're at touch four on a stalled deal, they need a strong proof piece, and they come up with nothing specific, nothing recent, nothing shaped like the prospect's situation. So they skip the touch, or they send something generic, or they paste in a bullet list of features nobody asked for.

The deal keeps sitting.

The fix isn't a project. You don't need a testimonial database or a case study production process or a dedicated marketing resource. You need a reflex. One small, automatic behavior that runs every time something good happens with a customer.

Here's what the reflex looks like.

When a customer says something good in conversation, you write it down before you hang up. Not "I'll remember this later" but actually putting words somewhere right now: what they said, who they are in general terms, what their situation looked like before, and what changed. Even a single rough sentence counts. "Client said the reopen questions brought back a deal they'd written off six months ago. Small agency, under ten people." That's a proof piece. It's not polished, but it's specific and retrievable, and you can use it.

When a customer leaves a review, you save it the moment you see it. Screenshot it or copy the text and drop it in a folder you can find in under a minute. Don't leave it sitting on the platform where you'll have to go hunting for it when you actually need it.

Every month or so, look at what you've collected and identify the two or three pieces that best match your current open deals. Pull those out and keep them somewhere accessible. The rest stays filed for future use.

That's the whole system. The capture reflex when something good happens, the save habit when a review arrives, and a monthly five-minute review to surface your most relevant active pieces.

The other piece is asking for proof directly. Most sellers are uncomfortable doing this. It feels awkward, like you're putting the customer on the spot. Chapter 17 goes into the exact questions that make the review ask and the referral ask feel natural rather than grabby. The short version for now: the right moment to ask is immediately after a customer tells you something is working. That's peak satisfaction. The ask at that moment doesn't interrupt anything. It extends a conversation that's already going well.

"Would you be willing to put that in a quick review? It would mean a lot."

At the right moment, that's enough.

The rep who builds this collection habit over six months operates differently than one who doesn't. She's not scrambling for something to send at touch four. She's choosing between three specific proof pieces and selecting the one that best fits this particular prospect. That's the position this chapter is designed to get you to.

Every happy customer is a future follow-up touch. Every result you capture now is a door that opens on a stalled deal later. The fifth conversation, the one your competitor never got to, sometimes reopens because someone who isn't you said the thing that finally made the prospect ready to move.

Build the habit of collecting that voice. Use it deliberately. And never assume that your own words, no matter how well chosen, are the only thing that can bring a conversation back to life.

Your Rep

The Drill.

Right now, go through your email history, your notes, or any customer messages you've saved and gather three proof pieces: a name, a number, and a story. They don't need to be polished. Rough notes are fine. Once you have three, pick the one that looks most like a deal in your pipeline that's been quiet for at least two weeks. Send it today as the entire reason for the touch. Two sentences on the situation, one sentence on the result, one connecting question at the end.

The Questions.

"Is this the same problem you're trying to solve?"

"What would a result like this change for you?"

"Want me to connect you with them so you can ask how it actually went?"

"Does this situation look anything like where you are right now?"

"Who on your side would feel this result the most directly?"

Train It.

The 90-day version of this drill is in The Fifth Conversation Workbook, at ConvoControl.com/fifthconversation.

Chapter Ten

Sound Human or Get Deleted

How long does it take you to spot an automated email? Two seconds? Your prospects are exactly as fast.

You feel it the moment you open it. The greeting is too smooth. The subject line is too clever. The first sentence compliments your company in a way that no human would ever write. You scan it for half a second and move on. Delete. Archive. Ignore. You don't even finish reading it.

Now flip that around. Your prospects are doing the exact same thing to your follow-ups. Every day, dozens of messages land in their inbox, all of them promising value, all of them sounding like they were written by the same robot, all of them going unread. The ones that slip through aren't the most polished. They're the ones that feel like a real person actually sat down and typed them.

That's the game right now. And you can win it without spending a dollar. You just have to sound like yourself.

The Bombardment

Your prospect's inbox is not what it was five years ago. Automation tools made it easy to send a thousand follow-up emails without writing a single new one. Artificial intelligence made it even easier, generating entire sequences that sound fluent and professional and completely lifeless. CRM systems fire messages on a schedule whether a human touches them or not.

The result? Your prospect is drowning.

They get cold outreach. They get re-engagement campaigns. They get newsletters they never signed up for, drip sequences from six different vendors, and automated "just checking in" messages from deals they thought were over. Some of it comes from bots pretending to be people. Some of it comes from real people who decided to let a bot do the work. From the prospect's side, it all looks exactly the same.

People adapt. They have to. They develop pattern recognition for machine-generated messages the way they develop pattern recognition for spam. They learn to dismiss a whole category of communication before they've even read the subject line. The filter isn't conscious. It's automatic, and it fires fast.

When that filter fires, your message is gone. Doesn't matter how valuable your offer is. Doesn't matter how good your timing was. Doesn't matter that you've been patiently working this deal for two months. If the message reads like it came from a sequence, it gets treated like it came from a sequence.

The good news is this: standing out has never been cheaper or easier. Everyone else is scaling the noise. You win by being the one message that obviously wasn't.

What Trips the Filter

If you want to avoid the delete reflex, you need to know what triggers it. These aren't subtle. Once you see them, you'll spot them everywhere, including in your own follow-ups.

The first trigger is the perfect greeting. "I hope this email finds you well." "Hope you're having a great week." "Trust this message finds you in good spirits." No real person writes that. A real person says "hey" or skips the greeting entirely and gets to the point. The polished opener signals automation before the prospect finishes the first line.

The second trigger is merge-field stiffness. "Hi {FirstName}, I noticed that {Company} has been expanding its presence in {Industry}." Even when the fields fill in correctly, it reads like a template because it is one. The sentence structure gives it away. Real messages don't sound like a form that got filled out.

The third trigger is length without reason. A real person following up on a specific conversation doesn't send five paragraphs. They send a line or two. When someone gets a long email from a seller they met once, they know the seller didn't write it specifically for them. Nobody writes five paragraphs to a single person unless they're billing by the hour.

The fourth trigger is the too-perfect cadence. Your prospect can't see your CRM, but they can feel it. When they get a follow-up exactly four days after the last one, then exactly seven days after that, then exactly ten days after that, the rhythm signals automation. Real people don't follow up on schedule. Real people send a message when something made them think of the other person.

The fifth trigger is corporate language. Words like "leverage," "synergy," "solution," "circle back," "reach out," "touch base," and "value proposition" belong in slide decks, not in a message from one human to another. When your follow-up sounds like a press release, it reads like nobody wrote it.

Run your last five follow-up messages through that list. How many of those triggers show up? For most sellers, the answer is uncomfortable.

How to Sound Human

The fix isn't complicated. It's specific.

Sounding human in a follow-up message comes down to one rule: say something only someone who was actually in the conversation would know. That's it. That's the whole secret.

You mentioned to your prospect that their board meeting was coming up and they were nervous about it. A human follow-up says: "how'd the board meeting go?" An automated follow-up says: "I wanted to reach out and see if there were any updates on your decision timeline."

You had a demo where their whole team was on the call and someone cracked a joke about their old software being older than their youngest employee. A human follow-up says: "hope you've been able to hold off on retiring that ancient system in the meantime." An automated follow-up says: "I'm following up on the demo we discussed and wanted to share some additional resources."

See the difference? One of those messages could have been sent to anyone. The other one could only have been sent to that person, about that conversation. The specificity is what sells it as real.

Short messages work. One to three sentences. Get in, make one point, ask one question, get out. A real text from a friend doesn't have five bullet points. It has one thought. Your follow-up can work the same way.

The subject line matters too. "Following up on our conversation" is the subject line of a sequence. "The board meeting" or "quick question about March" or no subject line at all reads like something a human sent. Pick the one that feels like how you'd start a text.

Reference the detail you would only know from actually talking to this person. Mention the thing they said was keeping them up at night. Bring up the internal deadline they told you about. Ask about the partner they were going to loop in. These are the notes you took during the conversation, and they're worth more in a follow-up than any feature list you could ever send.

One more thing: write the way you actually talk. Not the way you were trained to write in school. Not the way you'd write a proposal. The way you'd message someone you know. Contractions. Casual sentence structure. Maybe a sentence fragment here and there. That informality isn't unprofessional. It's human.

Imperfection on Purpose

Here's a counterintuitive move that works: let a little messiness in.

A perfectly formatted email with a perfectly structured body and a perfectly crafted call-to-action reads like something a machine produced, because machines produce perfect output. When a human types a quick follow-up, they start in the middle. They use lowercase. They send one thought without a subject line. They sometimes make a typo and leave it.

Imperfection is a signal. It says: I typed this right now, for you, on purpose. No sequence does that.

A voice note takes this further than any written message can. Record a thirty-second voice message, send it through a text or a LinkedIn message, and you've done something almost no other seller is doing. The prospect hears your voice. They hear your inflection. They hear that you're a real person who took real time to make something just for them. That warmth travels through audio in a way it can never travel through text.

Picture a rep, call her Keisha, who's been chasing a warm deal for six weeks. She's sent four emails, all polished, all professional, all unanswered. On the seventh week she pulls out her phone and records a twenty-second voice note: "Hey, Marcus, Keisha here. I know I've been sending you emails and you've probably been busy. I was thinking about our conversation from a few weeks ago where you said getting the new team onboarded was the priority. Just wondering if that's landed yet, or if it's still in progress. Let me know either way." That's it. She sends it. He responds within the hour. Not because the content was different from her emails. Because it felt like a person.

The lowercase text is another move worth knowing. No capital letters. No greeting. No sign-off. Just a quick message that reads exactly like something you'd send to a colleague. "hey, quick one: did the budget conversation happen yet?" That style signals immediacy. It signals that you didn't overthink this. It signals that you're a real person who was just thinking about them.

Perfect is suspicious now. Imperfect is proof of life.

This doesn't mean sloppy or careless. It means conversational. It means writing the way you'd talk. The rep who sends a two-sentence text that sounds like a person will generally outperform the rep who sends a six-paragraph email that sounds like a brochure.

Automate the Timing, Never the Voice

This is the rule that keeps everything honest. Write it down.

Automation is a tool. It exists to help you show up consistently, to remind you when a deal needs a touch, to keep the cadence without you having to remember everything in your head. That's the right job for automation. Use it for that.

The wrong job for automation is the actual message.

When you let a tool write and send the message on your behalf, you're not following up. The tool is following up. And prospects can feel the difference. They're not reading your words. They're reading the words of a system that's optimized for open rates and click-through, not for the specific conversation you had with a specific person about a specific problem.

The person who controls the conversation controls the outcome. You can't control a conversation you handed to a machine.

Let the CRM remind you. Let the calendar alert fire. Let the sequence tell you it's time to reach out. That's smart. That's how you stay consistent on a full pipeline without anything falling through the cracks. But when that reminder fires, you show up. You. Not a template with your name on it. You open the contact, you think about the last conversation, you write something that only you could write, and you send it.

A tool that sends messages pretending to be you is wearing your name badge. It's making commitments you don't know about. It's building (or destroying) a relationship without you in the room. The prospect thinks they're talking to you. They're not. When the conversation gets real, that gap shows, and it costs you the deal.

There's also an ethical side to this worth naming. Your follow-up system should reflect who you actually are. If you're the kind of professional who pays attention, who remembers details, who shows up for the people you're trying to serve, then your follow-ups should look like that. If your messages sound like a bot, people assume you're a bot. And bots don't close deals. People close deals, because everything is a conversation, and conversations require two actual humans.

Set up the system to remind you. Set aside the block (you'll build that in Chapter 15). And then when it's time to reach out, be there. Actually there. Write the message yourself. Keep it short. Keep it specific. Keep it real.

That's the whole thing. The reps compound. The relationship builds. The deal stays alive. And when the fifth conversation finally happens, it happens because you were the one rep who was always actually in the conversation.

The Standout Math

Think about the math for a second.

Your prospect is getting flooded. On any given day, a busy professional with an active vendor relationship might get ten, twenty, maybe thirty automated follow-ups from various sellers. All of them sound roughly the same. All of them are easy to ignore. The delete reflex fires, and they're gone.

Now you send one message. It's short. It's specific. It mentions the exact thing they said in your last conversation. It asks one real question. It comes from a person, not a sequence.

That message has almost no competition. Because nobody else is doing it.

This is the leverage play of this whole chapter. You don't have to be smarter than everyone else. You don't have to have a better offer or a lower price or more features. You just have to sound like a person. In a world full of automated noise, that's genuinely rare. And rare gets read.

Personalized messages that reference specific prior conversations dramatically outperform templated ones. The gap isn't small. It's not a slight edge. Personalization is the whole game now, because automation has made the non-personalized message essentially invisible.

You trained for this. You took notes in the first conversation. You logged the details. You know what matters to this specific person. Now use it. Every follow-up is a chance to demonstrate that you were actually listening, that you actually care, and that you're actually different from every other seller in their inbox.

That's a competitive advantage nobody can buy. A vendor can copy your price. They can copy your product features. They can copy your proposal format. They cannot copy the fact that you were actually present in the conversation and you actually remember what was said.

Sound human. Get read. Stay in the deal.

Your Rep

The Drill. Pull up your next scheduled follow-up, whether it's sitting in a draft, a CRM task, or your calendar. Before you send it, run it through the five filter-triggers from this chapter: perfect greeting, merge-field stiffness, too long, too-perfect cadence, corporate language. If it trips even one, cancel the automated send and rewrite it by hand. Reference one specific detail from your last real conversation with that person. Keep it to two or three sentences. Add one question at the end. Send that version instead.

The Questions.

"Does this read like I typed it to this specific person, or like something I sent to a list?"

"What did they say in our last conversation that I could reference right now?"

"What's the one thing this person would immediately recognize as something only I would know?"

"Would they be able to tell this message was written for them, and only them?"

"If I got this message in my own inbox, would I read it or delete it?"

Train It. The 90-day version of this drill is in The Fifth Conversation Workbook, at ConvoControl.com/fifthconversation.

Chapter Eleven

Text Beats Voicemail: Pick the Weapon

When did you last listen to a voicemail from a number you didn't know? Exactly. So why are you still leaving them?

That's not a rhetorical jab. It's a genuine question worth sitting with. Because most sellers default to the phone call, leave a voicemail when nobody answers, and then wait. And wait. And get nothing back. And then wonder what went wrong.

What went wrong is channel mismatch. You chose your comfort zone, not their inbox.

Channel strategy isn't glamorous. Nobody gets fired up about picking between text and email. But match the wrong medium to the wrong moment, and your follow-up disappears entirely. Match it right, and that message gets read in under three minutes.

This chapter is about picking the right weapon for the right fight. Because the system built in every chapter before this one, the questions, the value touches, the reopen lines, all of it only works if the message gets read. And the message only gets read if it shows up in the right place at the right time.

The Response-Rate Reality

Let's settle one thing fast. This isn't about personal preference. It's arithmetic.

Think about your own behavior for a second. When your phone buzzes with a text, how long before you glance at it? Most people pick it up within a few minutes. The message is short. Easy to scan. Easy to reply to.

Now think about voicemail. When you see a missed call from a number you don't recognize, followed by a voicemail notification, what do you do? Most people ignore it. Some listen a day or two later. A few never listen at all. They just wait to see if the person texts, or they look the number up and decide it's not worth calling back.

Study after study on business communication puts text open rates in a completely different universe than voicemail retrieval. The gap isn't close. Text wins by a wide margin, almost every time, for almost every buyer type.

Phone calls from unknown numbers get screened. This isn't new. It's been true for years, and it's gotten worse as robocalls have trained everyone to let unknowns go straight to voicemail. The moment your prospect sees an unfamiliar number lighting up their screen, they've already made a decision. And it isn't "I should answer this."

Voicemail has another problem on top of the screening issue. Even when someone listens to your message, there's no easy way to respond. They have to call you back, which means carving out time, remembering the context, and being ready for a full conversation. That's friction.

A text lets them reply with two words in fifteen seconds while they're standing in line for coffee.

This is why channel choice matters more than most sellers realize. You can write the perfect message, send it at the perfect time, with the perfect opening question, and still get zero response if you put it in the wrong container.

The highest-paid skill in follow-up isn't what you say. It's knowing where to say it.

Think about it from a training standpoint. You can practice a technique perfectly in the dojo, but if you execute it at the wrong moment in a match, it doesn't score. Timing and placement are part of the skill. Channel selection is timing and placement for your follow-up.

Here's what most sellers miss. The follow-up system in this book is only as good as the delivery. You can't control a conversation you can't get into. And you can't get into a conversation if your message never gets read. Channel selection is the door. Everything else is what happens once you're inside.

So before you draft your next follow-up, ask yourself one question: where does this person actually live? Not where you're most comfortable reaching out. Where do they show up, respond, and engage? That's where your message goes.

What Each Channel Signals

Every channel sends a signal before the message even starts. You need to know what signal you're sending, because the medium shapes the mood before the prospect reads a single word.

A phone call says: this is urgent. Or I think it's urgent. It asks the person to stop what they're doing right now and give you their full attention. It's a demand on their time, even when it's framed as friendly. For established relationships or high-stakes moments, that signal fits. For a routine follow-up after one meeting? It often comes across as pressure, even when none is intended.

A text says: I'm thinking of you, but I'm not going to take over your day. It's low friction. It reads in seconds and takes seconds to reply to. It signals closeness without demanding immediacy. When used right, a text feels like a tap on the shoulder from a colleague, not a knock on the door from a stranger.

An email says: there's something here worth your time, and you can get to it when you're ready. Email signals detail and documentation. It's easy to save, easy to forward, easy to reference later. It's also easy to defer, which is why emails sit unopened while texts get answered. For things that need to be in writing, email is the right call. For re-engaging a stalled deal, it's often the wrong tool because it gives the prospect permission to put you off.

A video message says: I went out of my way for you. A thirty-second video is so rare in most sales relationships that it stops people. They watch it. The warmth of a face and a voice carries more weight than any written message, and the effort signals genuine investment. It's rare enough to stand out and personal enough to get a reply.

A message on LinkedIn or a comment on their content says: I'm paying attention to your world. It's low pressure, keeps you visible, and meets them inside a platform they already use for business.

None of these is universally right. The question is always the same: what signal does this moment need?

If the deal is hot and moving fast, a call makes sense. If you haven't heard back in a week and want a low-friction nudge, text. If you need to send a revised proposal, email. If you want to cut through the pile of automated sequences flooding their inbox, record a quick video.

Choose the signal on purpose. The rep who picks a channel randomly leaves that decision to chance. The rep who matches the medium to the moment controls the conversation before it even starts. The person who controls the conversation controls the outcome, and that starts before you type the first word.

Earning the Right to Text

Text is your most powerful follow-up channel. It's also the most personal. That combination means you can't just start texting someone because you have their number. That's the fastest way to feel like an intrusion.

You have to earn the right.

Earning it is simple. Ask for it in the first conversation. One question, asked naturally near the end: "What's the best way to reach you, call or text?"

That's it. Most people will tell you directly. Some prefer email. Some prefer text. Some give you both options and tell you which they check more often. The act of asking does two things that matter.

First, it tells you their preferred channel, so every follow-up you send lands in a place they actually check. Second, it signals that you're going to follow up. You're not sneaking up on them later. You're being upfront about the fact that this conversation continues, and you want to reach them the right way when you come back. Most buyers respect that. It reads as organized and professional.

Once someone says "text is fine" or "yeah, text me," that permission changes the entire game. Your texts arrive from a contact they're expecting to hear from. They don't have to wonder who you are. They know. And because they said yes to the channel, they're already a little more inclined to reply.

There's another way to earn texting rights that feels even softer. Near the close of the first meeting, offer to text them a quick recap. "Mind if I text you a summary so it's easy to find later?" People almost always say yes to that because it's helpful and it costs them nothing. Now you've sent a text they were expecting, your name is in their messages, and the next text lands like a continuation of something already in progress.

Never cold-text someone who hasn't given you permission. Even if you have their number, even if it's listed publicly somewhere, starting with an uninvited text feels invasive. The bar for this channel is higher than for email because it's more personal. Respect that line, and the channel rewards you. Cross it, and you lose the contact entirely, often permanently.

Think of earning the right to text the way you'd think about earning access to any tool in training. You don't walk into a new gym and immediately start using the advanced equipment. You show up, do the work, build the relationship with the space, and earn each tool as you're ready for it. Get the meeting. Run the conversation. Ask for the channel. Then use it well.

One more thing. When you earn permission to text, use it sparingly enough that it stays valuable. A text a day turns high-open into ignored. One well-timed, well-crafted, single-question text every few days or every week keeps the channel warm without wearing it out.

The Channel-Matching Rule

Once you know which channels a person uses, one rule makes your follow-up system almost foolproof: follow up on the channel they last answered on.

This sounds obvious. It is obvious. Almost nobody does it consistently.

Here's what happens in practice. Picture a rep, call her Dana. She sends an email after a strong first call. No reply. She sends a second email. No reply. She calls and leaves a voicemail. No reply. Then, almost as an afterthought, she sends a casual text. The prospect replies within five minutes.

What did Dana learn? She learned which channel that person actually lives on. And from that moment forward, she has one job: text.

The channel they answered on is the channel where you have permission and presence. Go back to that one. Stop spreading touches across every possible medium hoping one sticks. Find the groove and stay in it.

The same logic applies in reverse. If someone replies to your emails at 6am, that's data. It tells you they're in their inbox early, probably before their day gets loud. Send your next email at 5:55am. Meet them in their groove.

This is the channel-matching rule: stop following up in the place that's comfortable for you and start following up in the place where they actually show up. The deal lives in their world, not yours.

One practical habit that makes this easier: when someone responds to any touch, note the channel and the time in your CRM or follow-up log. It takes ten seconds. Over time, those notes build a picture of exactly when and where each person in your pipeline is reachable. That picture is worth real money. It's the difference between a follow-up system that feels like guesswork and one that feels almost surgical.

Every time a prospect responds, you get a rep. Every rep teaches you more about how to reach them. You store that information, and you fall back on it the next time. That's training. That's the system working.

The Pattern Interrupt and B2B vs. B2C Maps

Here's the one exception to the channel-matching rule, and it's important.

When a channel goes dead, switching channels is the move.

Three unanswered emails, or three unanswered texts, or three voicemails with no reply, that's a signal. The channel isn't working. Something changed. Maybe they got slammed at work. Maybe your messages are getting filtered. Maybe they moved to a different device and that inbox isn't getting checked. Whatever the reason, continuing to knock on the same locked door is stubbornness, not persistence.

Switch channels. One short text after three unanswered emails lands like a tap on the shoulder. It interrupts the pattern, both the pattern of your sends and the pattern they've fallen into, which is ignoring your emails without really deciding to. A text arriving in a different context, from the same person, at the right moment, can restart a conversation that email never could.

Keep the interrupt short. No setup, no apology for not hearing back, no "hey, just circling back on my emails." Just a single direct question that stands on its own. Something like: "Still thinking through whether this makes sense for Q3?" That's it. Short, human, and carrying exactly one question, as covered in chapters 11 and 4.

Now, the B2B and B2C maps. Because where your message goes depends heavily on the type of buyer you're reaching.

Corporate buyers are professionals inside companies with IT policies, shared inboxes, and a culture of asynchronous communication. Email is often their primary work tool. They use it, they're used to it, and they respond to it during business hours. LinkedIn is relevant because they're there for business anyway.

Reach them mid-week, mid-morning. That's the strongest default for this group. Avoid Monday morning, which is consumed by catch-up and fire-fighting. Avoid Friday afternoon, which is mentally already the weekend.

Texts can work for corporate buyers, but usually only after rapport is established. Earn it with a business-case reason ("mind if I text you the link so it's easier to find?") before going conversational.

Business owners are on their phones constantly. They're moving, making decisions, and handling small emergencies all day long. Email is often where things go to wait. Texts get seen.

Try early morning before their business opens, or early evening after close. Those are the windows where they're not mid-operation and their brain has room for a reply. Phone calls work better for owners than for corporate buyers, often because owners are used to running their businesses on calls and don't screen as aggressively. But timing still matters. Mid-rush, when they're managing staff or customers, isn't the window.

Consumers live their lives in the evenings and on weekends. After 5pm, when someone is home and the workday pressure has dropped. Saturday morning, when the week's noise has settled. Text is the dominant channel here because that's where personal communication happens. Nobody is doing their personal thinking in a corporate inbox.

Respect the clock. Reaching a consumer at 2pm on a Tuesday when they're at work doesn't just get ignored. It can actively create friction because it puts your message in the wrong context.

Map every open deal to one of these types: corporate buyer, business owner, or consumer. Then map that type to the right channel and the right window. Write it in your notes. Check it before you send.

The rep who shows up at the right place at the right time, with the right question, in the right format, is the rep whose follow-ups get answered. Every other variable in this system gets amplified when the delivery is right.

Channel is the container. Make sure the container matches the person who's opening it.

Every message you send is a small test of whether you've been paying attention. The prospect doesn't fill out a form telling you their preferences. They reveal them through their behavior. A reply to a text tells you something. An email answered at 6:30am tells you something. A voicemail that gets called back tells you something. Listen. Log it. Use it.

The fifth conversation is out there waiting. In a lot of cases, the only thing standing between you and that conversation is sending the next touch through the right door.

Your Rep

The Drill. In your next live conversation with a prospect, ask permission to text before the call ends. Use the first question below. Then, within 24 hours of that conversation wrapping up, send your first follow-up as a one-question text. Keep it under two lines. Make it human. End it with a single question that's easy to answer in seconds.

The Questions.

"What's the best way to reach you, call or text?"

"Mind if I text you the recap so it's easy to find?"

"quick one: did the numbers land with your partner?"

"Still thinking through whether this makes sense for Q3?"

"You mentioned things get crazy in October. Has it settled a little?"

Train It. The 90-day version of this drill is in The Fifth Conversation Workbook, at ConvoControl.com/fifthconversation.

Chapter Twelve

Questions That Reopen Doors

The deal went quiet three weeks ago. You're staring at a blank message. What do you type?

That's the moment this chapter was written for. Not the strategy, not the mindset, not the principle. The actual words. The cursor is blinking. The prospect hasn't replied in weeks. You know something needs to go out, but you don't know how to start.

Most sellers freeze here and then never send anything at all. Or they default to the worst possible openers because those are the ones sitting at the top of their mental library, the ones they've seen a hundred times in other people's emails. "Just checking in." "Any update?" "Bumping this to the top of your inbox."

Those don't work. We'll get into why shortly.

What works is a question matched to exactly where the deal sits right now. Not where it was three weeks ago. Not where you want it to be. Where it is. A depth-appropriate question, sent in the right channel, from a person who sounds like an actual human being, reopens doors that have been quietly closing.

This chapter is the toolkit. Dog-ear it. You'll come back to it.

Openers by Depth

The biggest mistake sellers make when reopening a stalled deal is treating all silence the same. Three days of quiet and three months of quiet are not the same thing. The appropriate question for touch two is completely different from the appropriate question for touch nine. Using the wrong depth for the moment is like showing up to a first practice in sparring gear. It signals you don't read the room.

Think of opener depth in three levels.

Touch two: momentum questions. You just had a good conversation. The energy was there. They were engaged. Then a week passed and you haven't heard back. This isn't a ghost situation. This is normal deal rhythm. Your question should ride the energy of the last conversation, not start from scratch.

Momentum questions are light and assumptive. They assume forward motion. They don't ask whether the deal is alive. They assume it is and pick up where you left off.

Questions to train with at touch two:

"How did the internal conversation go after we talked?" (Use this when they said they needed to loop in a partner or team member. It assumes the conversation happened and asks what came from it.)

"Did you get a chance to pull those numbers we talked about?" (Use this when they mentioned they were going to look into something specific. It follows their thread, not yours.)

"What stood out to you most after you had time to think it over?" (Use this when the first meeting ended well and you want to find out what landed. It invites reflection without demanding a decision.)

"Has anything changed on your end since we talked?" (Use this when time has passed and you want a soft check-in that gives them room to surface any new information without pressure.)

"Where are you at on this after sitting with it for a bit?" (Use this when you want a status without making it feel like an interrogation. The phrase "after sitting with it" acknowledges that they've been thinking, which respects their process.)

These questions work at touch two because they're gentle, they reference the last conversation, and they give the prospect something easy to respond to. They're not asking for a decision. They're asking for an update on thinking that's already in motion.

Touch five: status questions. You've followed up a few times now. Some touches got replies, some didn't. The deal is still alive but it's slowing down. At this depth, you shift from momentum to location. You need to know where the deal actually sits right now, because something may have changed that you don't know about yet.

Status questions are honest and direct. They locate the deal without being aggressive.

Questions to train with at touch five:

"Is this still on your radar for this quarter, or has it moved to the next one?" (Use this when timing is the most likely variable. It gives them two clear options and both are acceptable, which lowers the pressure to respond.)

"What's the current priority level on this compared to when we first talked?" (Use this when you suspect other things may have moved in front of yours. It opens the door for them to be honest about where you rank.)

"Where does this sit with you right now on a scale of one to ten?" (Use this when you want a temperature read without a long conversation. A short number answer is easy to give and tells you a lot.)

"Has something come up that's shifted the timeline?" (Use this when silence started after a specific moment, like a company event, a hiring change, or a major announcement. It creates space for them to share context they may have been reluctant to bring up.)

"Is the decision on this still yours to make, or has it moved to someone else?" (Use this when there's any chance the internal ownership of the deal has changed. Nothing stalls a deal faster than chasing the wrong person.)

Status questions work at touch five because you've earned the right to be direct. You've shown up multiple times. You've delivered value. A straight question at this point isn't pushy. It's professional.

Touch nine: honesty questions. You're deep into the follow-up now. This deal has been quiet for a while. You've been patient. You've sent value. You've tried multiple channels. At touch nine, the most respectful and effective move is frank honesty. These questions give the prospect full permission to tell you the truth, whatever that is.

Questions to train with at touch nine:

"Should I take this off my active list, or is there still something worth pursuing here?" (Use this when you genuinely don't know whether the deal is alive or dead. It's not a threat. It's an invitation to be straight with you.)

"I've been following up because I believe this could be a real fit. Does that still feel true on your side?" (Use this when you want to restate your genuine belief in the fit without restating your pitch. It puts the question back on them.)

"What would need to change for this to become a real conversation again?" (Use this when you suspect the deal is stuck on a specific obstacle they haven't named. It invites them to name it without you having to guess.)

"If we're honest with each other, where does this stand?" (Use this when everything else has been tried. It's a peer-level question that signals you're not going anywhere but you also respect their time too much to keep guessing.)

Honesty questions work at touch nine because the polite dancing has run its course. A prospect who is still reachable after nine touches either has genuine interest that's been buried under life, or they've been too polite to say no. Either way, a direct question gets you out of limbo faster than another soft nudge.

Surfacing the Real Stall

Here's a hard truth about stalled deals. The reason a prospect goes quiet is almost never the reason they gave you when things slowed down.

"We need to think about it" rarely means they're thinking about it. "The timing isn't right" often means the budget got cut or the decision got pushed to someone else. "We have a lot going on right now" almost always means something else moved to the top and your deal got buried under it.

None of this is deception. Prospects aren't usually lying to you. They're giving you the surface answer because the real answer feels awkward to say out loud. "Honestly, my boss killed the budget" is a harder thing to say than "the timing's just not great right now."

Your job at this stage is to create a question that makes the real answer feel safe to give.

The key question at the heart of this section is: "Is the holdup the money, the timing, or something nobody's said out loud yet?"

Train with variations of it. The exact wording matters less than the structure. You're giving them a menu of honest options, including the catch-all at the end that gives permission for any answer they might have been afraid to say. That third option, "something nobody's said out loud yet," is the one that unlocks the real conversation more often than the first two.

Other variants to have in your arsenal:

"On a practical level, what's the one thing that would need to be different for this to move forward?"

"If I'm being direct with you, what's actually in the way?"

"You've been thoughtful throughout this process. What's your honest gut on it?"

The pattern in all of these is the same. You're lowering the cost of honesty. You're signaling that you can handle the real answer and that you'd prefer it to polite vagueness. Most buyers, when given genuine permission to be straight, take it. And once you know the real stall, you can either address it or move on. Both are better than guessing.

What you never want to do is send a follow-up that requires the prospect to work hard to respond. A vague message about "just checking in on things" gives them nothing to react to. But a specific question about a specific obstacle gives them something concrete to engage with, even if the answer is "yeah, that's still the problem."

The rule here: name the most likely stall in your question. Don't be afraid of it. Naming it doesn't make it more real. It just makes it discussable.

The Assumption Flip

This is one of the most effective moves in the reopen toolkit, and it takes about ten seconds to execute.

Instead of asking an open-ended question about where the deal stands, state the pessimistic assumption and let them correct you.

People often correct wrong assumptions faster than they answer open questions. It's a common impulse. When someone says something we know to be untrue or incomplete, we feel the need to respond.

Use this to your advantage.

"Should I assume the timing's wrong and close the file on this?" lands differently than "Where does this deal stand?" The first one requires a reaction. The second one invites silence.

More questions built on the assumption flip:

"If I haven't heard back, I'll assume you've gone another direction. Is that the case?" (This creates gentle urgency without pressure. The prospect doesn't have to reply to agree. But most will reply to correct you if you're wrong.)

"Based on the silence, I'm guessing something came up on your end that made this less urgent. Fair?" (This is generous. It gives them a face-saving explanation and invites them to confirm or redirect.)

"I may have missed the window on this. Has the conversation moved on without me?" (This is humble and specific. It acknowledges the possibility that decisions happened without you, which is sometimes exactly what occurred.)

The reason the assumption flip works so consistently is that it removes the pressure of a direct question while creating a different kind of pressure. The prospect isn't being chased. They're being given a chance to set the record straight. And if the record needs setting, they'll usually take it.

One important note. Keep the assumed pessimism honest. Don't overstate it to manufacture urgency. "I guess you just don't need this anymore" is different from "I'm assuming the timing shifted." The first is passive-aggressive. The second is professional. The goal is to create a comfortable opening for correction, not to guilt someone into replying.

Used right, the assumption flip is one of those moves that feels almost too simple. It works because it respects the other person's intelligence and their time. It says: I know something might have changed. I'm not going to pretend otherwise. Here's my best read. Tell me if I've got it wrong.

Their Own Words as the Master Key

Every prospect tells you something in the first conversation that unlocks every follow-up that comes after. You just have to write it down.

The most powerful reopen question you'll ever send isn't one you made up. It's one they gave you, reflected back in their own words.

"You mentioned in our first conversation that budget decisions for Q4 get made in September. Is September here yet?" can't be confused for a mass email. It can't be mistaken for an automated sequence. It could only have come from someone who was actually in that conversation, actually listening, actually paying attention.

That's the master key. Their own words, returned to them with a question attached.

Here's how to build it. During every first conversation, you're listening for three types of statements: timelines, obstacles, and priorities. A timeline is anything that anchors the decision to a future point in time. "We'd need to have this figured out before the holidays." "We're mid-migration right now." "We're waiting on Q3 results." An obstacle is anything that's currently in the way. "We need budget approval." "My partner needs to see this." "We're tied up with a hiring freeze." A priority is anything they say matters most to them about the problem.

"Speed is the biggest thing for us." "The team has to actually use it or it doesn't matter." "We've been burned before by overpromising ven dors."

Log all three. Write them down during or immediately after the conversation. They don't need to be perfect quotes. Just accurate summaries.

Then, when you reopen the deal, open with one of those statements.

"You said if the pilot went well, we'd talk rollout. How did it go?" cannot be ignored the way a generic follow-up can. It obligates a response because it proves you were listening. It makes the prospect feel seen. And it picks up the thread of their own story, which is always more compelling than your pitch.

More examples of how this looks in practice:

"You told me the team was stretched thin through the end of the quarter. Is the dust settling?" (Timeline, returned.)

"You mentioned your partner hadn't been brought in yet. Did you get a chance to loop them in?" (Obstacle, followed up.)

"You said speed was the biggest thing. Is that still where it sits?" (Priority, revisited.)

This technique is also why taking notes during a first call is a trained skill, not a nice-to-have. The rep who takes no notes walks into the second conversation blind. The rep who wrote it all down walks in carrying the prospect's own words. Those are different salespeople having completely different conversations.

If you've already had the first conversation and didn't write anything down, go from memory. What do you remember? Even a partial quote is better than a generic open. "You had mentioned something about a system migration. Is that still in progress?" uses the memory of their words without claiming perfect recall.

The goal is to show up like someone who was paying attention. Because the fifth conversation is built on every exchange that came before it. The details you gathered in conversation one are the raw material for conversations two through five.

What Never to Open With, and Your Personal Top Ten

Three phrases disqualify your follow-up before the prospect reads the second word. You've probably sent all three. Everyone has. This is where we fix it.

"Just checking in." This opener says nothing. It gives the prospect nothing to react to, no question, no value, no reason to engage. It also signals low confidence, as if you're apologizing for reaching out. No one replies to "just checking in" because there's nothing to reply to. There's no question, no conversational ball to catch. It's a statement about your behavior, not an invitation to theirs.

"Any update?" This one is slightly more direct but still fails for the same core reason. It puts the entire burden of the conversation on the prospect. They have to generate the response from nothing. If they had an update they wanted to give you, they probably would have already. Asking "any update?" rarely surfaces one.

"Bumping this to the top of your inbox." This line was clever the first time someone wrote it. That was years ago. Now it signals a sequence, not a human. The moment a prospect reads "bumping this," they know it's automated. They know it's template number four. And they delete it, or ignore it, without guilt.

Each of these fails for the same reason: no question, no value, no reason to reply. They're touches in form only. They don't advance the conversation, and advancing the conversation is the only thing a follow-up is supposed to do.

Replace every one of them with a single specific question from the depth levels covered earlier in this chapter.

Now, the personal top ten.

By the end of this chapter, you should be building your own list of ten reopen questions, written in your own words, for your specific market. Not a list to memorize and recite. A list to train with, adapt, and have ready so you never stare at a blank message again.

Here's how to build it.

Take two questions from touch-two momentum openers. These are your post-first-call questions, the ones you'll reach for when the deal is fresh and you want to keep energy alive.

Take three questions from touch-five status openers. These are your mid-process questions, the ones that locate the deal honestly after a few exchanges.

Take two from touch-nine honesty openers. These are your deep-patience questions, the ones that create space for real answers when polite conversation has run its course.

Take one assumption flip. This is your pattern-interrupt question, built for the moment when direct questions haven't worked.

Take two built from their own words. These are custom to your most common prospect types and the most common things your buyers tell you in first conversations.

Write all ten in your own language. The questions in this chapter are reps to train with, not lines to lift. What works in your market, in your voice, for your type of buyer, is what belongs on your list. Someone selling enterprise software needs different depth-five questions than someone selling coaching services. Someone working with small business owners needs different momentum questions than someone working with hospital procurement teams.

The framework is universal. The words are yours.

Most people read. Few people rep. The reader who builds this list, keeps it somewhere visible, and uses it on real deals in the next week is operating at a different level than the reader who moves on to the next chapter with good intentions. Build the list today.

Your Rep

The Drill. Pull three stalled deals from your pipeline right now. Place each one at a depth: early quiet (touch two range), mid-stall (touch five range), or long silence (touch nine range). Then write one reopen question for each deal, using the appropriate depth level from this chapter. Send all three today. Log every reply you get.

The Questions.

"When we talked in May, getting off the old system was the priority. Is it still?"

"Has this dropped down the list, or off it?"

"What would make this a yes at some point, even if that point isn't now?"

Train It. The full reopen-question toolkit is in the free template pack at ConvoControl.com/fifthconversation.

Chapter Thirteen

When They Ghost

They loved the demo. They asked for the proposal. Then: nothing. What happened?

You replay the call. It went well. The energy was there. They asked the right questions. They said "send it over" with actual enthusiasm. And now your proposal has been sitting in their inbox for two weeks without a word.

You send a follow-up email. Nothing. You call. Voicemail. You send another email, shorter this time, because you read somewhere that shorter is better. Nothing.

This is the ghost. And it's one of the most disorienting experiences in sales because you don't know whether you lost or just haven't won yet. The silence tells you nothing. Or so it seems.

The silence actually tells you quite a lot. You just have to know how to read it.

This chapter is the silence playbook. It breaks down what different kinds of quiet actually mean, how to interrupt patterns that have gone dead, and exactly what to say when you need a response but can't get one. It also covers the most important skill of all: knowing when to genuinely stop.

Decode the Silence by Stage

Not all ghosts are the same. When someone goes quiet depends heavily on what the silence means, and that meaning shifts based on where you were in the deal when the quiet started.

Ghosted early, after the first conversation. This is the most common kind of silence and the least alarming. You had a strong first call, maybe even said "send me the information" and they meant it at the time. Then life hit. Something more urgent landed on their desk. A fire started somewhere in their business. You slipped from the front of the queue to the middle.

The mistake most sellers make with early ghosts is treating the silence as a signal to try harder. They send longer emails, more detailed follow-up, additional resources, a second proposal. All of that adds to the pile the prospect already isn't getting through. Less is more here. One short, specific, easy-to-answer question. That's the move.

Ghosted late, after multiple exchanges. This kind of silence is a different animal. You've had several conversations. Things were moving. Then something shifted and the communication stopped. This usually means something changed internally that you don't know about yet.

Common culprits: a key stakeholder changed their mind or left the company. A budget got cut or reallocated. A competing priority arrived that your solution can't solve. An internal champion who was driving the deal lost internal support. A competitor stepped in with a better offer, a better relationship, or a better price.

Late-stage silence calls for a more direct approach. You've earned the right to ask a straight question. Something from the touch-five or touch-nine range in chapter 12, a question that acknowledges the silence and invites honesty about what changed. The goal is to surface the real obstacle, because whatever changed is the thing you need to know about.

Ghosted after the proposal. This is the most psychologically specific kind of silence, and it has three distinct causes.

Sticker shock. The proposal came in higher than they expected, and they don't know how to have that conversation. It's easier to go quiet than to say "this is more than we budgeted."

Internal politics. Someone inside their organization pushed back, and your champion is navigating that conversation without telling you they're navigating it. They'll come back when there's something to report. Or they won't.

Fear of the no conversation. Some buyers genuinely dislike delivering bad news. They know they're probably not going to move forward, but saying that out loud to you feels uncomfortable. So they delay. And delay. And delay.

Each of these calls for a slightly different question. Sticker shock: "I want to make sure the numbers make sense for where you are. Is the investment the part that needs another look?" Internal politics: "Is there someone else on your side I should be talking to?" Fear of the no conversation: "If the answer is no, that's completely fine. Is it no?"

Reading the stage correctly tells you which door to knock on. Knock on the wrong door long enough and you're just making noise.

The Pattern Interrupt

When a channel goes dead and a deal goes quiet, you need to change something. Sending the same kind of message through the same channel expecting a different result is one definition of doing it wrong.

The pattern interrupt is a deliberate break in the rhythm, designed to land differently than everything you've already sent.

Here's how it works. You've sent three professional, well-crafted, single-question emails. No reply. Your next move is not a fourth professional email. Your next move is something that catches them off guard in the best possible way.

Change the channel. As covered in chapter 11, three unanswered emails are a signal to switch. A short, human text after three silent emails lands like a tap on the shoulder. They've been passively ignoring your emails the way we all passively ignore things we're not ready to deal with. A text puts you in a completely different context, a more personal one, and that context shift triggers a fresh read.

Change the length. If your emails have been two or three paragraphs, try one line. Literally one line with one question. The brevity itself communicates something: you're not demanding much, you're not overwhelmed them, and you haven't given up. One line is easy to answer. It's harder to scroll past than a wall of text.

Change the tone. If your previous messages have been professional and slightly formal, try something more casual. Lower your own register. Write the way you'd text a colleague, not the way you'd write a memo.

Now, humor. Used carefully, a light touch of humor can humanize your follow-up in a way nothing else can. The keyword is carefully. One line, self-deprecating, never sarcastic about their silence. Something like: "I'm starting to worry I said something wrong. Did I say something wrong?" works because it's light, self-aware, and prompts a smile before it prompts a reply. It doesn't guilt them. It doesn't pressure them. It just makes them feel okay about responding.

The trap with humor is overuse. One light line in an otherwise brief message works. A joke-heavy email reads as desperate. Keep it to one moment of warmth, not a stand-up set.

What you're doing with the pattern interrupt is interrupting the category your messages have fallen into inside their head. They've unconsciously filed your previous emails under "that thing I'll get to eventually." A different medium, a different length, or a different tone forces a re-categorization. You're not the same email they've been not opening. You're something new that arrived unexpectedly.

The pattern interrupt doesn't always work. Some deals are genuinely done and the prospect is just too polite to say so. But the interrupt almost always produces a data point. A reply, any reply, tells you where you are. Even a "sorry, we went another direction" is infinitely more useful than silence, because it frees you to move on.

The Takeaway

When you hold on tight, prospects go quiet. When you open your hand, they come back.

The takeaway is not a dramatic breakup email with a subject line that reads "Closing the file on your account" and seven paragraphs about how you tried so hard. That kind of email gets forwarded around offices with an eye-roll. It reads as a manipulation technique because it is one, and experienced buyers recognize it immediately.

The real takeaway is something much simpler and much more honest.

"Should I close the file on this?"

That's it. One question. Seven words. It works for a specific reason: it costs the prospect almost nothing to answer and it costs them something real to not answer.

If the deal is genuinely dead, they can reply with "yes, sorry for the delay, we went a different direction" and feel like they've done you a courtesy. That's an easy reply. Almost no effort.

If the deal is alive but buried, "should I close the file?" prompts action. They don't want you to close the file. They have to do something to prevent that outcome, which means they have to reply. The question creates low-stakes urgency that pressure and deadlines can't create.

And if they don't reply at all, you have your answer. A prospect who doesn't respond to "should I close the file on this?" is a prospect who has made their decision through silence. That's a clean answer. Move on

.

Variations that train well alongside the core question:

"Is this dead, or just buried under everything else?" This one is warmer. It gives them a face-saving option. "Buried" is sympathetic. Most people would rather say "buried" than "dead."

"If the answer is no, that's completely okay. Is it no?" This is the most permission-giving version. It removes every trace of pressure by explicitly saying no is acceptable. When a buyer feels like no is acceptable, they're far more likely to tell you the truth. And sometimes the truth turns out to be a qualified yes.

What all three share is honesty and respect. They don't pretend the silence isn't happening. They don't manufacture urgency. They simply ask for a straight answer in a way that makes giving one easy.

Send the takeaway question once. Don't follow it with a second one. The power of this question is its finality. If you send it and then send another follow-up three days later before they've had a chance to reply, you've undercut the whole thing. Send it. Wait. Give it real space.

When to Actually Stop

At some point, continuing to follow up isn't persistence. It's noise. Knowing the difference is a skill.

Here's the clearest signal that it's time to genuinely stop: the takeaway question got silence too.

You sent "should I close the file on this?" You waited a full week. Nothing came back. That silence is an answer. Not every answer arrives as words.

When that happens, do two things.

First, move the deal to the long-game list covered in the next chapter. Not every "no" is permanent. Not every silence means forever. Circumstances change. Budgets open. Leadership shifts. Problems get urgent that weren't urgent before. A deal that's quiet today can reopen in six months when the conditions change.

Second, send one final note. Not a question. Not a follow-up. Just a short, clean, human message that leaves the door open without standing in it.

Something like: "Totally understand if the timing isn't right. I'll be here when it makes sense to pick this back up. Take care."

That's not a guilt trip. It's not a placeholder for a future push. It's a professional close that leaves the relationship intact. Because the relationship outlives the deal. Always.

How you exit a conversation is as important as how you entered it. A prospect who felt respected even when they didn't buy, or didn't buy yet, is a prospect who thinks of you first when the circumstances change. A prospect who felt pressured, guilted, or harassed at the end might buy from you never, even if the fit is perfect.

Exit with grace. Leave the door open. Move on to your active pipeline and let the long-game system do its work.

One more thing about knowing when to stop. Be honest with yourself about why you're continuing to follow up. Is it because there's genuine evidence the deal is alive? Or is it because you've invested time in it and you don't want to let go? Those are very different reasons. The first justifies continued effort. The second is a sunk cost, and sunk costs don't close deals.

The trained rep knows the difference. They keep pursuing what has life and release what doesn't. That discipline, the willingness to let go, frees up time and energy for the deals that are actually moving.

The Graveyard Revival Play

Here's a quarterly habit worth building that pays for itself every time.

Once every ninety days, pull up your oldest ghost files. The deals that went silent months ago. The ones you moved to the long-game list and haven't looked at since. Pull the ten oldest ones, and send each of them the takeaway question.

"Should I close the file on this?"

That's still the question. Even six months later. Even a year later.

The reason this works is simple. Circumstances change faster than most sellers account for. A deal that was completely dead eight months ago may have changed shape dramatically since then. The company got funding. The champion got promoted and now has budget authority. The competitor they chose didn't deliver and they're in the market again. The project that pre-empted your deal finished, and now there's bandwidth.

Any of those changes can happen with no notice to you. The prospect isn't going to call you unprompted to say "hey, things have changed, let's talk again." They're busy. They've moved on in their heads. You're not on the top of their list.

But a simple, respectful question arriving at the right moment can reconnect everything instantly.

Picture this composite situation. A rep sends the revival question to twelve old ghosts in one afternoon. She gets two replies that same day. One says "actually, yes, please close it, we handled it differently." Clean. Done. Moved on. The other says "funny you should write, we've actually been talking about this again. Can we get on a call this week?"

That second reply is the deal that makes the whole habit worth it. It's also the deal that her competitor, the one who stopped following up six months ago, will never get.

The graveyard revival play works for two reasons. One, it catches the deals that reopened without announcement. Two, it clears the dead weight from your long-game list so you're not tracking deals that have genuinely closed without you. Both outcomes are valuable. You either get a conversation back or you get clarity.

Run the revival play once a quarter without fail. Block thirty minutes, pull the list, send the question. The habit costs almost nothing and produces outsized returns over the course of a year.

The fifth conversation doesn't always happen on the schedule you expected. Sometimes it happens fourteen months after the first one, when a revival question lands at exactly the right moment. That conversation counts just the same.

Your Rep

The Drill. Go into your CRM or your notes right now and find your five oldest ghost deals. Not your active stalls. The ones you stopped following up on. The ones you haven't touched in months. Send each one the closing-the-file question today. Keep the message short. Let the question do the work. Then log every reply you receive.

The Questions.

"Should I close the file on this?"

"Is this dead, or just buried under everything else?"

"If the answer is no, that's completely okay. Is it no?"

Train It. The 90-day version of this drill is in The Fifth Conversation Workbook, at ConvoControl.com/fifthconversation.

Chapter Fourteen

The Long Game

Where do your "next year" deals go? If the answer is "nowhere, really," this chapter pays for the book.

Most sellers treat "call me next year" as a soft no. They thank the prospect, close the laptop, and move on to the next fresh lead. The deal disappears from the active list, and with it, all the work that went into getting that first conversation.

That is not a qualified no. That is an invitation with a timestamp. And the seller who treats it as an invitation will be there in October when the budget opens. The seller who treated it as a soft no will be competing for a new first conversation while someone else is already in conversation five.

The long game is a pipeline. It's just a pipeline with a longer clock. And almost nobody tends it.

The Long Game as an Asset

A well-kept not-now list is a pipeline your competitors don't know exists.

Read that again. While every other rep in your market is fighting for new first conversations, you have a list of people who already said yes to talking to you, who already expressed real interest, who told you their timeline, and who are now just waiting for the right moment. That list is invisible to your competition. They can't prospect into it. They can't outbid you for it. The only way to build it is to stay in the game long enough to earn it.

Deals close in month eleven all the time. They just don't close for the rep who disappeared in month one.

Here's what happens when a long-game prospect is ready to buy. They've been thinking about the problem the whole time. It never fully went away. Then something changes, the budget frees up, the Q3 results come in, the pain gets too loud to ignore, and they're suddenly ready to have a real conversation. At that moment, one of two things happens. Either they remember someone who stayed in touch with them, who showed up quarterly with something useful, who treated the relationship like it was worth maintaining even when there was no deal on the table. Or they go back to Google and start over.

The first outcome goes to the rep who played the long game. The second outcome gets expensive for everybody.

Think of the long-game list the way a coach thinks about player development. Not every athlete is ready to compete at the top level right now. Some are still growing into their strength. That doesn't mean you drop them from the program. You keep working with them. You check in. You develop the relationship. And when they're ready, you're the first person they call because you're the only one who was there the whole time.

Your not-now list is your development roster. Tend it.

The Quarterly Value Touch

Once a quarter. Every long-game prospect. One touch. One question.

That's the whole system. It's almost embarrassingly simple. Which is probably why almost nobody does it consistently.

The quarterly value touch keeps you real in someone's mind without crossing into noise. Monthly is too often for a genuinely dormant deal. You'll wear out your welcome. Yearly is too infrequent. A lot can change in a year, and if you only show up once, you're likely to miss the window when things shift. Quarterly hits the right rhythm. It says "I haven't forgotten about you" without saying "I'm desperate."

The content of the quarterly touch matters as much as the timing. It can't be a naked follow-up with no substance. "Just checking in to see if next year is here yet" is annoying. It has all the same problems as the openers covered in chapter 12. No question, no value, no reason to reply.

Every quarterly touch delivers something from your value bank, as built in chapter 8. A relevant insight about their market. A short piece of proof from someone in a similar situation. A question that advances their thinking on the problem they originally came to you about. One of those three, every time.

Here's what a good quarterly touch looks like in practice. Picture a rep, call him Paulo. He has a prospect who said "budget's frozen until Q2" seven months ago. Every quarter since, Paulo has sent something brief and useful. First quarter: a short note about a trend in their industry, ending with "curious if you're seeing this on your side." Second quarter: a summary of how a company in a similar situation handled the same problem, ending with "does this match where you are?" Third quarter, which is now: "Q2 came and went. Has the budget situation shifted?"

Paulo didn't pitch. He didn't pressure. He didn't remind the prospect that he was still waiting. He just kept showing up with something worth opening. And now, in the third quarter, when he asks the direct question, the prospect doesn't feel ambushed. They've been in a relationship with Paulo all year. The question is natural.

That's the goal of the quarterly value touch. By the time you ask the direct question, the relationship has already been rebuilt through the work of staying present.

One practical note. You don't have to write a custom value piece for every long-game prospect every quarter. That would take forever. Your value bank, the one from chapter 8, is designed to be reused. Pick one insight, one proof piece, or one question that's relevant to a cluster of your long-game prospects. Personalize the opening line. Send it to all of them. The personalization in the first sentence makes each message feel individual even when the core content is shared.

"Thought of you when I saw this" does a lot of work. It signals attention without requiring you to write a brand-new message from scratch for every single contact.

Trigger Events

The quarterly touch is the baseline. But the moves that often reopen deals the fastest aren't scheduled. They're triggered.

A trigger event is any change in your prospect's world that makes the problem you solve more urgent, more relevant, or newly possible to address. These events happen constantly. Most sellers miss them entirely because they're not watching.

Here are the most common triggers to monitor.

New funding. A company that just raised money suddenly has capital it didn't have before. Your solution, which was previously impossible to budget, is now in play. The congratulations message lands easily here: "Saw the announcement on the funding round. Congrats. Does this change the conversation we started back in the spring?"

A new role. A contact who moves into a bigger role, or moves to a new company entirely, is a trigger in two directions. At their new organization, they have fresh authority and probably fresh problems. At their old organization, there's a new person in the seat who may be looking to make changes. Both are openings.

"Congrats on the new position. Curious if the problems you were solving before followed you to the new role, or if there's a fresh version of them to work through?"

A new fiscal year. This is the most predictable trigger of all. The moment a new fiscal year opens, budgets reset and priorities reshuffle. If you know a company's fiscal year calendar, you can time a touch for the first week of their new year almost every time. That message lands when they're actually in the headspace of deciding what to invest in.

A competitor stumbling. If you sell in a competitive market and one of the major players has a visible problem, an outage, a scandal, a price increase, a bad round of reviews, that's a trigger. Your prospects who use that competitor are suddenly thinking about alternatives. A light, non-gloating message acknowledging the situation and asking an open question can restart conversations that had been fully closed.

"Noticed there's been some noise around [competitor's situation]. If you're rethinking any of your current setup, happy to revisit the conversation we had last year."

No gloating. No "I told you so." Just a calm, useful presence at the right moment.

A regulation or seasonal change. Depending on your market, changes in law, compliance requirements, or seasonal business rhythms can dramatically shift urgency. A rep selling into healthcare, finance, or any regulated industry should be watching the regulatory calendar the same way they watch a prospect's fiscal year.

How do you watch for trigger events? Set alerts. Google Alerts for company names, LinkedIn notifications for key contacts, industry news subscriptions. It takes about twenty minutes to set up and then runs in the background indefinitely. The information flows to you rather than requiring you to go hunting for it.

The trigger event touch isn't a follow-up in the traditional sense. It's a relevance moment. You're showing up because something changed in their world, not because a calendar date reminded you to reach out. That distinction matters. Prospects can feel the difference between a scheduled sequence and a genuine response to their news. The second one gets opened. The first one gets deleted.

The System That Never Forgets

Here's the most important sentence in this chapter.

If a "call me next year" lives in your head, it's already gone.

Memory is not a follow-up system. Memory is unreliable, contextual, and easily overwritten by the next urgent thing. You cannot run a long-game pipeline in your brain the same way you cannot run a training program by remembering to practice when you feel like it.

The system has to remember so you don't have to.

Every "call me next year," every "check back in Q3," every "we're not ready until the migration is done," gets logged the moment it's spoken. Not after the call. Not when you get back to your desk. The moment it's spoken.

Log three things for every long-game prospect: the trigger (what they said has to change before they're ready), the date (when that change is expected to happen), and the reopen question you'll use when you come back (using the words they used, as covered in chapter 12).

The tool doesn't matter. CRM, calendar, a paper notebook, a recurring reminder in your phone. Use whatever system you'll actually maintain. Complexity is the enemy of consistency. A simple note in your calendar that fires three days before the prospect's stated timeline is infinitely more valuable than a sophisticated CRM that you never open.

What matters is the logging reflex. The moment a "not yet" lands, the log entry gets made. The moment the log entry gets made, the deal is still alive in your system even if it's dormant in your mind.

Picture two reps hearing the same thing from a prospect: "We need to wait until after the merger closes, probably around February." Rep one nods, says they understand, ends the call, and moves on. By October, the prospect is a blurry memory in a long list of deals that didn't go anywhere. Rep two logs it immediately: trigger is merger closing, expected date is February, reopen question is "last time we talked, you were waiting on the merger to close. Did it?" In February, rep two is there. Rep one isn't.

The fifth conversation sometimes happens in February, fourteen months after the first one. It only happens for the rep whose system remembered.

Build the habit now, before you have too many long-game deals to track by memory. The reps who build this habit early, when it's easy, are the ones who have a thriving not-now pipeline in year three that their competition can't touch.

The Compounding Effect

Here's what the long game looks like from month fourteen.

You've been sending quarterly touches to a prospect for a year. Four messages. Each one delivered something useful. Each one ended with a light question. Three of the four got a brief reply. One was a warm acknowledgment. One answered your question with a quick update. One said "still not quite ready but I appreciate you staying in touch."

That last reply is the one that matters most. It tells you the prospect hasn't written you off. It tells you they see value in the relationship even when there's no transaction happening. And it tells you that when the moment comes, they're going to think of you first.

By month fourteen, something interesting happens. You are the only rep still standing there. Everyone else who pitched this prospect, and there were others, has long since moved on. Their sequences ended, their follow-up dried up, they cycled to new prospects. You stayed.

And the trust built by simply showing up quarterly is trust no pitch can buy. This is the compounding effect. The longer you maintain the relationship without asking for anything, the more valuable your eventual ask becomes. When you finally say "I think now is the time," it lands with the weight of a year of consistent presence behind it.

The gymnastics parallel here is real. A coach who shows up every day, gives useful feedback, stays patient through the plateaus, earns a different kind of trust than the one who only appears before competitions. The athlete who trains with the consistent coach performs differently when it counts. The long-game seller who showed up every quarter earns a different kind of relationship than the one who sprinted hard for a month and disappeared.

Consistency is the credibility. It's the proof that you mean what you say, that you believe in the fit, and that you're not going to vanish after the check clears. Buyers know that about you before the deal closes because they watched you for a year.

The long game also has a practical compounding effect in your pipeline. The rep who tends a not-now list consistently has a second pipeline that closes throughout the year on an unpredictable schedule. Some months the fresh leads are slow. But a long-game conversion that month keeps the number healthy. Over a year, the not-now list functions as a pipeline buffer, a source of deals that opens and closes on its own timeline, independent of your prospecting rhythm.

That buffer has value that's easy to underestimate when you're looking at a single month. Look at a full year and the picture changes. The rep with a well-tended long-game list closes deals in months where other reps are panicking about pipeline. The source of those deals is invisible to most observers. It looks like luck. It's not. It's the compound interest on a year of showing up.

One more thing. The prospect who buys in month fourteen also tends to be a particularly good customer. They've been watching you for a year. They know what they're getting. The relationship is already established. The trust is already built. Implementation tends to be easier. Retention tends to be higher. The lifetime value of a long-game conversion can outpace the lifetime value of a quick close, because the foundation is so much stronger.

Tend the long-game list. It's the pipeline nobody sees, and it's the one that quietly changes careers.

Your Rep

The Drill. Build your long-game list today. Go through your CRM, your email, your notebook, and anywhere else deals might be hiding. Find every "next year," "not now," "check back in Q3," and "we need to wait until." For each one, log the trigger, the expected date, and the reopen question in your own words. Then schedule one quarterly touch for each deal, starting from today's date. Put it on your calendar. Block the time.

The Questions.

"You said next year. It's next year. Where does this sit now?"

"Congrats on the funding round. Does this change the conversation we started?"

"Still watching this space for you. Has anything shifted?"

Train It. The 90-day version of this drill is in The Fifth Conversation Workbook, at ConvoControl.com/fifthconversation.

Chapter Fifteen

Consistency Is the Skill

What's your follow-up routine? Not your intentions. Your routine.

Not the follow-up system you mean to run. Not the cadence you described to your manager. The actual thing you do, at the same time, in the same way, every single day.

Most sellers pause at that question. Not because they don't know the answer. Because the answer is "I don't really have one." There are intentions. There are bursts of activity after a good training call or a slow month. There are weeks where follow-up is relentless and weeks where it falls off the edge of a full calendar. But a routine? A daily practice? Something that happens whether motivation shows up or not?

For most people, that doesn't exist yet.

This chapter builds it.

Everything in the previous fifteen chapters is knowledge. This chapter turns knowledge into behavior. Because a follow-up system you run once a month when you feel like it isn't a system. It's a mood. And moods are the worst possible thing to run a sales career on.

Consistency Beats Intensity

Here's the uncomfortable math that most sellers never run.

A frantic burst of touches, then radio silence, then another burst when you panic, produces worse results than a solid, valuable touch every single week.

Study after study on behavior change, habit formation, and skill development lands in the same place: the performer who trains consistently over time outperforms the one who trains hard occasionally. This is true in athletics. It's true in music. It's true in medicine. And it is absolutely true in sales. [2]

The gymnastics parallel is direct here. In competitive gymnastics, you don't win on a routine you practiced once with full intensity. You win on a routine you've done so many times that the body executes it correctly under pressure without conscious thought. The routine that you've run a thousand times in practice is the one that holds up when the judges are watching. The one you ran hard for a week? It falls apart under the lights.

Follow-up works the same way. A prospect who hears from you consistently, at a predictable rhythm, with something useful every time, builds a picture of you over months. That picture is reliability. It's the professional who says what they'll do and then does it. That impression can't be created in a sprint. It's built touch by touch, over time, by showing up.

The sprint also creates an unintended signal to the prospect. When you disappear for three weeks between bursts, they notice. Not consciously, usually. But the inconsistency registers. It suggests that you're reactive, that you follow up when you're desperate or when something prompted you to, not because you have a system and you care. Buyers are more perceptive than sellers give them credit for. They feel the rhythm, and an erratic rhythm doesn't inspire confidence.

Sales rewards the metronome. The consistent, steady, reliable presence is the one that earns trust. The sprint earns a few replies when it happens, then silence when it stops.

If there's one mindset shift that separates the sellers who have strong pipelines year-round from the ones who have great months followed by dry months, it's this. The strong-pipeline sellers aren't necessarily more talented. They're more consistent. They show up every day. The daily habit is the competitive edge that most people refuse to build because it sounds boring.

It's not boring. It's how professionals play.

The Daily Follow-Up Hour

One protected block. Same time every day. Phone silenced. Follow-up is the only job inside that block.

That's the structure. It's not complicated. Complexity is the enemy of consistency, so the structure has to be simple enough that nothing about it requires a decision on the hard days.

One hour. Same time. Every day.

The specific time matters less than the specificity. Pick a time slot that you can protect, and protect it. A lot of sellers do their follow-up block in the morning, before the day's reactive demands take over. Others do it right after lunch, when the morning sprint has cleared and there's an hour before the afternoon picks up. Some do it at the end of the day, as the last thing before they close the laptop. Any of those works. What doesn't work is "whenever I get to it," because "whenever I get to it" means it doesn't happen on the days it most needs to.

Inside the block, follow-up is the only job. No email monitoring. No checking notifications. No quick tasks that "only take a minute." The block is sacred in the same way a training session is sacred. You don't stop a training session to answer texts. You train.

Here's what a healthy pipeline actually needs every day, expressed in terms of touches. If you're working twenty to thirty active deals, you need to send somewhere between five and ten touches inside that daily block to stay on top of cadence. Not all twenty to thirty deals need a touch every day. But if you're scheduling touches properly, as covered in chapter 8's Follow-Up Ladder, a meaningful number of them will be due any given day. That's what the block handles.

For smaller pipelines, ten to twenty deals, the block still happens. It might only produce three or four touches on a given day. That's fine. The habit is what matters, not the volume. The block exists whether the pipeline is full or thin, because a thin pipeline is partly a result of not running the block consistently.

Inside the block, work from your calendar and your pipeline list, not from memory. Memory is where follow-up goes to die. The previous chapter covered why: if a deal lives only in your head, it's already gone. The block is when you execute what the system has already scheduled. Open the calendar, find the touches due today, execute them in order.

Phone on silent. Laptop notifications off. This isn't an aesthetic preference. It's operational necessity. Research on focus and interruptions is consistent: a single interruption takes several minutes to recover from. An hour of interrupted follow-up is functionally much less than an hour. Protect the block the way a surgeon protects an operating room. Nothing comes in that isn't already on the table.

What Kills the Block

If the block is so valuable, why do most sellers not have one?

The answer is almost always the same: the reactive morning.

Here's how it usually goes. You open the laptop intending to do your follow-up. But first you check email, just to see if anything urgent came in overnight. There are twelve emails. A few need quick replies. One has a question that requires a document. One is a complaint that needs to be handled. One is from your manager asking for an update on three deals, which means you need to pull the information, think through each one, and write a response. By the time you surface from the inbox, forty-five minutes have passed and the follow-up block hasn't started yet.

Then a meeting runs long. Then a call comes in. Then there's a problem that only you can handle. By the time it's all quiet again, the day has evaporated, and the follow-up goes on the list for tomorrow.

Tomorrow, the same thing happens.

This is not laziness. This is the structure of a reactive workday. When you let the inbox set the agenda, you're prioritizing everyone else's urgency over your own high-value activities. Email is, almost by definition, other people's priorities arriving at your desk. Opening it first means starting the day already behind on your own work.

The fix is structural, not motivational. Block first, inbox second.

This means the follow-up block happens before you open email in the morning. Before you respond to last night's messages. Before you see what the day has decided it wants from you. You protect the first hour, or whatever window you've chosen, for the work that doesn't arrive in your inbox because nobody is sending you deals to follow up on. You have to create those conversations yourself. That requires a protected time with no incoming fire.

"But what if something urgent arrives overnight?" Most things that feel urgent in an inbox at 8am are not actually urgent. They can wait sixty minutes while you do the work that drives your income. If something is genuinely emergency-level urgent, someone will call you. Let the block run first.

The reactive morning is a habit. Inbox-first is a habit. Breaking it requires a deliberate choice, made every day, until the new pattern takes over. That takes longer than most people expect and shorter than most people fear.

Set up the block before you go to sleep tonight. Put it in the calendar. Put it in tomorrow's calendar. And then when tomorrow morning arrives, run the block before you touch the inbox. See what the day looks like when you start it on offense.

Streak Mechanics

Habits have a fragile early period. In the first week or two of building the follow-up block, the behavior isn't automatic yet. It still requires a deliberate choice. The streak is the tool that carries you through that period.

Track consecutive days. A simple count of how many days in a row you've completed the block. Day one, day two, day three. You can track it with a paper calendar and a pen mark, a habit-tracking app, a note in your phone, or a sticky note on the desk. The tool doesn't matter. What matters is that you can see the number.

Here's why the number matters. By day seven, something psychological shifts. Breaking the streak has a cost. You've built something. Stopping now means starting over from zero. That cost, small as it sounds, is often just enough friction to make you run the block on the days motivation doesn't show up.

And motivation doesn't show up every day. This is the part that nobody tells you when they talk about habits. There are days when the prospect list feels like a wall. Days when every message you draft feels wrong. Days when you'd rather do anything other than follow up on stalled deals. Those days exist for everyone. The difference between the seller with a routine and the one without is simple: the seller with a routine does it anyway.

You don't rise to the occasion. You fall back on how you've trained.

This is the core of the athletic philosophy behind everything in this system. The gymnast who's trained the routine ten thousand times doesn't need to feel ready on the day of the competition. The training runs the routine. The musician who's practiced the piece for months doesn't need inspiration on the night of the performance. The practice carries the performance. The athlete who's done the conditioning doesn't need motivation on race day. The conditioning does the work.

Same thing here. When the routine is built and the streak is real, the follow-up block happens because the block always happens at this time, on this day, and you've done it enough times that not doing it feels wrong. The mood is no longer a factor. The system decides.

The never-break-it-twice rule is the safety mechanism for streaks. You will miss a day. Travel, illness, an emergency, a day that genuinely swallows everything. When that happens, let it happen without guilt and start again immediately. The rule is not "never miss a day." The rule is "never miss two days in a row." One missed day is a blip. Two missed days is the beginning of a pattern. Don't let it become a pattern.

When you restart the streak after a break, restart from one. Don't try to compensate for the missed day by doing extra the next day. Just run the block, mark day one, and build from there. The streak will get back to where it was faster than you expect.

The Identity Close

There is a point, reached after enough daily follow-up blocks, where something subtle changes.

You stop thinking of follow-up as something you do and start thinking of it as something you are.

This is the identity shift. It's the most durable form of a habit there is.

Before the identity shift, every block is a choice. You're choosing to do follow-up today. Some days that choice is easy. Some days it takes effort. After the identity shift, the block is just part of how your day runs. You do it the way you brush your teeth. Not because you feel inspired to. Not because the numbers are good. Because this is what you do, and who you are, and how you operate.

The rep with a follow-up routine doesn't have to feel like following up. The athlete doesn't have to feel like training. The routine decides, not the mood.

This sounds abstract until you've experienced it. Once you have, it becomes the clearest possible explanation for why some sellers seem to produce consistently across good months and bad ones, across motivated periods and flat ones, across winning streaks and losing streaks. They're not winning because they feel great. They're winning because their system runs regardless of how they feel.

When a deal comes in from the long-game list, or a ghost replies after six months, or a stalled deal reopens because of a quarterly touch that landed at exactly the right moment, it doesn't feel like luck. It feels like the natural result of showing up every day. Because that's exactly what it is.

The rep who has done fifty straight days of the follow-up block has sent hundreds of touches. Some landed and some didn't. But the ones that land are landing in a pipeline that's been tended consistently, and the results look completely different from the pipeline that's worked in bursts.

These are the reps you build in the daily block. These are the exact habits trained one-on-one in the mastery program, until they're not habits anymore. Until they're just how you operate.

The fifth conversation doesn't happen because you were inspired that day. It happens because you showed up every day, and one of those days was the day the prospect was finally ready.

Your Rep

The Drill. Block the same 60 minutes every day for the next two weeks. Pick the time right now, before you close this chapter. Put it in your calendar. Repeat it for fourteen consecutive days. Follow up only inside that block. Count your touches at the end of each block and write the number down. Track your streak.

The Questions. Ask yourself these at the end of every block:

"Did I train today?"

"How many conversations did I keep alive today?"

"What's my streak?"

Train It. Want these reps trained into you one-on-one until you can't get them wrong? That's the Black Belt mastery program. The application lives at ConvoControl.com/fifthconversation.

Chapter Sixteen

Track It or Lose It

What's your actual average touch count on closed deals? If you don't know the number, you're training blind.

Think about that for a second. You've read fifteen chapters about a follow-up system. But do you know, from your own data, how many touches your closed deals actually took? Do you know which channel got the most replies last month? Do you know how many deals in your pipeline died from silence on your side?

Most sellers don't. They feel their way through follow-up based on instinct, mood, and a general sense of whether things are going well or not. That works sometimes. It works the way playing a sport without ever watching the tape works. You improve, slowly, based on general experience. But you miss the specific patterns that could double your performance in half the time.

The scoreboard changes that. Five minutes a week is the whole cost. The payoff is a follow-up system that gets sharper every month because you can actually see what's working.

Why Tracking Is Non-Negotiable

The principle is simple. What gets measured improves. What doesn't, quietly dies.

This isn't a sales concept. It's a universal truth about human performance. Athletes track their splits, their reps, their margins. Surgeons track outcomes by procedure and by provider. Coaches track win-loss records, individual player metrics, and team tendencies by quarter. Every serious discipline has a scoreboard, because without a scoreboard you're guessing.

Most salespeople work in a profession that rewards performance financially, sometimes dramatically, and yet most salespeople track almost nothing about their own behavior. They track revenue, usually because their company forces them to. They might track pipeline in a CRM, usually because their manager asks for it. But their personal follow-up behavior? How many touches a closed deal takes on average? Which opener questions get replies? Which channel is generating the most conversation? Almost nobody is tracking that.

The result is a career built on folklore. "I followed up a lot and it worked." "That prospect just wasn't ready." "My product sells itself." These explanations feel true. They're not evidence. They're stories told in the absence of data.

The scoreboard replaces folklore with evidence. And evidence is the only thing that lets you make targeted improvements rather than general effort.

Here's the practical argument. Say you know from your own data that texts get answered three times more often than emails in your specific market. Armed with that information, you adjust your channel strategy immediately. Every stalled deal that's been getting emails starts getting texts instead. The math changes overnight, not because you worked harder, but because you stopped doing the thing that wasn't working and did more of the thing that was.

You can only make that adjustment if you tracked it.

Five minutes a week. That's the whole investment. Not a reporting system. Not a complex dashboard. One simple habit of recording what you did and what came back. The compound interest on that habit over twelve months is a follow-up system that's been tuned to your specific market, your specific buyer, and your specific voice. That's a competitive advantage nobody can copy because it's built from your data.

The Four Numbers

The scoreboard tracks four numbers. Just four. Any more than that and the tracking becomes the job, which defeats the purpose.

Number one: touches per closed deal.

This is your personal proof that the fifth conversation is real. For every deal you close this year, count the total number of touches it took from first conversation to close. Log that number. Over time, average it.

This number will surprise you. Most sellers, when they actually count, find their average is higher than they thought on deals they closed, and much lower than it needed to be on deals they lost. The closed deals took six, eight, ten touches. The lost deals got two or three and then silence.

That's not a coincidence. That's the math of chapter one made personal. Your own closed deals are the most persuasive evidence you'll ever have that staying in the conversation longer works. Not a study. Not a book. Your own results.

Once you know your true average touch count on closed deals, you have a benchmark. On any given stalled deal, you can look at where you are in the touch count and ask: have I actually given this deal a fair shot? If your average close takes eight touches and you're on touch three, the answer is no. You're not behind. You're not even at the midpoint yet. Keep going.

Number two: reply rate per touch type.

Every touch you send belongs to a category: email, text, call, LinkedIn, video. Within email and text, you can further track by question type if you want more granularity, but start with channel.

Each week, note how many touches went out in each channel and how many got a response. Even a rough count. Over four to six weeks, a pattern will emerge. One channel will consistently outperform the others. That's your channel. Move more touches there.

This number also teaches you about timing. If you're tracking when your touches go out and when replies come back, you'll start to see that certain time windows produce better response rates. An email sent at 7am might get answered by 9am. The same email sent at 2pm might not get answered at all. That's a small adjustment with compounding returns.

Number three: deals revived from silence.

Every time a ghost replies, every time a graveyard revival play produces a response, every time a takeaway question reopens a conversation, log it. This number tracks the payoff of all the patience and consistency built over previous chapters.

It's easy to feel like the revival plays are low-percentage moves. That the graveyard is mostly dead weight. But once you track how often the "should I close the file on this?" question produces a reply, or how often the quarterly touch on a long-game prospect kicks off a real conversation, the picture changes. What felt like a long shot becomes a reliable part of the system.

This number also builds the habit of running revival plays consistently. When you can see that your last quarterly sweep produced three conversations, running the next quarterly sweep feels less like hope and more like execution.

Number four: deals lost to no follow-up.

This is the hardest number to look at. And the most important.

At the end of each month, review the deals that went cold or officially died. For each one, honestly answer: did they say no, or did I stop asking?

Some deals will be genuine losses. The prospect made a decision, they went another direction, the timing was never going to work. Those are real losses. Log them as such.

But some deals, look honestly, will be deals you abandoned. Deals where the last touch was yours and there was never a reply telling you no. Deals where the prospect went quiet and you let the quiet become permanent. Those are not losses. Those are abandonments. Log them separately.

Over months of tracking, the ratio of losses to abandonments tells you something specific about your quit behavior. If you're abandoning more deals than you're losing, your quit number from chapter one is still too high and the daily block from chapter sixteen isn't running yet. If the abandonments are shrinking, the system is working.

This number is uncomfortable because it requires honesty. But it's the single most actionable piece of data on the scoreboard. You can't fix what you won't measure.

What the Numbers Teach

The four numbers, tracked consistently, teach you things about your follow-up game that no amount of instinct and guesswork ever could.

Your true quit point versus your close point. This is the gap. The average touch count on closed deals is your close point. The average touch count on abandoned deals is your quit point. If your quit point is three and your close point is seven, the entire system is telling you one thing: keep going past three. The next four touches are where your income is. You now know that because you can see it in your own data.

Your best channel. Not the channel you prefer. The channel where your specific buyers, in your specific market, with your specific communication style, actually reply. Your instinct says calls are best because you're more comfortable on calls. Your data might say texts get answered twice as often. Follow the data.

Your best send windows. When do replies actually come back? Early morning? Lunch? Tuesday versus Thursday? The scoreboard shows you. Most sellers are surprised to find their reply-generating window is narrower than they thought, and landing in it consistently changes the numbers.

Which questions outperform. If you're tracking which opener questions get replies, you'll find that some consistently outperform others with your specific buyer type. The assumption flip might work brilliantly in your market and fall flat with a different one. The "is this buried or off the list?" question might produce replies at a higher rate than "where does this sit on your priority list?" You can only know which is true for you if you track what you sent and what came back.

The scoreboard turns opinion into evidence. And operating from evidence, in a game where most people operate from opinion, is a meaningful edge.

The Simple Scoreboard

The scoreboard doesn't need to be complicated. Complicated tracking systems don't get used. Simple ones do.

Here's a layout that works on paper, in a spreadsheet, or inside whatever CRM you're already using. Five columns. That's all.

Column one: deal name or contact name. Column two: touch count this week. Column three: channel used. Column four: reply received (yes or no). Column five: notes on what was sent and what came back.

At the bottom of the page, a small summary section with this week's totals.

Total touches sent. Total replies received. Reply rate (replies divided by touches). Channel breakdown (how many touches per channel, how many replies per channel). Deals revived this week. Deals abandoned this week.

That's the full scoreboard. It takes about five minutes to fill in at the end of each daily block, or ten minutes to fill in at the end of the week from your sent messages and notes.

Here's what filling it in looks like with a composite week. Say you sent fifteen touches. You used email nine times, text five times, and left one voicemail. Replies came back on six touches. Five of the six replies came from texts or emails. The one voicemail produced nothing. Three deals moved forward. One deal got the takeaway question and replied to say yes, close the file. One ghost from three months ago replied after a revival question and asked to schedule a call.

Now look at what that week's scoreboard tells you. Your reply rate is roughly 40 percent. Texts and emails produced replies. The voicemail produced nothing. One deal closed off the long-game list. That's a good week. And you know exactly why it was a good week, which means you can repeat it.

Next week's plan: no voicemails, more texts, keep running the revival plays. That's not a vague intention. That's a specific adjustment based on real data.

Imperfect data beats no data. You don't need perfect records or a sophisticated system to start. A piece of paper and a pen work. Whatever you track, even roughly, is more than you knew before. Start there, and the system will get more accurate over time.

The Review Ritual

Five minutes. Every Friday. That's the review ritual.

At the end of every work week, before you close the laptop, you look at the scoreboard for the week and answer three questions. What worked? What didn't? What changes Monday?

What worked is anything that produced a reply, moved a deal forward, or revived a conversation. Name it specifically. "Texts on Tuesday morning produced three replies." "The assumption flip question on the Garcia deal got a response after three silent emails." Specific is useful. General is decoration.

What didn't work is anything that got no traction. Three emails to the same channel that produced nothing. A question you sent five times this week across five different deals and heard nothing back on. A channel you tried for the first time that fell flat. Name those specifically too.

What changes Monday is the adjustment. One or two things, not five. Small course corrections every week beat grand resolutions every quarter. If texts are outperforming emails, you shift the ratio slightly toward texts next week. If Tuesday mornings are producing more replies than Thursday afternoons, you move some touches to Tuesday morning. If the assumption flip question is outperforming open questions, you use it more.

Over twelve months of this, the follow-up system that emerges is nothing like the generic one described in the earlier chapters. It's yours.

It's built from your data, tuned to your market, and calibrated to how your specific buyers respond. Nobody else has that system because nobody else has your data.

The five-minute Friday review is the refinement mechanism. The daily block is the engine. The four numbers are the fuel gauge. Together, they turn follow-up from something you do by feel into something you run by evidence.

And evidence, applied consistently over time, closes deals.

The fifth conversation doesn't happen because you guessed right. It happens because you tracked what worked and kept doing it.

Your Rep

The Drill. Build your scoreboard right now, before you do anything else. Use paper, a spreadsheet, or your CRM. Set up the five columns. Then go back to last week's activity, even roughly, and fill in what you can remember. Count the touches, note the channels, mark the replies. Get a number on the page, even an imperfect one. Imperfect data today beats perfect data never.

The Questions. Ask yourself these every Friday:

"What's my real average touch count on closed deals?"

"Which touch type got answered this week?"

"How many deals died this month from silence on my side?"

Train It. The one-page scoreboard is in the free template pack at ConvoControl.com/fifthconversation.

Chapter Seventeen

Follow-Up After the Yes

You closed. Congratulations. Why are you disappearing NOW?

The deal is signed. The payment processed. You've moved on to the next prospect, the next first conversation, the next pitch. You earned it. You did the follow-up, you stayed in the conversation longer than everyone else, and you got the yes.

And now, almost without thinking about it, you've gone quiet on the person who just gave you money.

This is one of the most expensive habits in sales and one of the most common. Most sellers treat the close as the finish line. It's not the finish line. It's the starting line of an entirely different race. The one where you get referrals, reviews, repeat business, and the kind of word-of-mouth that no advertising budget can buy.

Everything is sales, because everything is a conversation. And the conversation with a customer doesn't end at the close. It shifts. The seller who understands this, and follows up on the yes the same way they followed up on every "not yet," builds something that looks less like a pipeline and more like a flywheel.

Why Sellers Vanish After the Close

The disappearance happens for a few reasons, most of them understandable.

Momentum pulls you forward. The close was the goal. Achieving it sends your attention immediately to the next goal. The deals still working in the pipeline are urgent. The new customer is handled. This is how it feels, anyway.

There's also a subtle fear that reaching out after the close might feel like hovering, or like you're waiting for a complaint to arrive. Some sellers unconsciously avoid post-close contact because they don't want to prompt second-guessing. If the buyer is happy, why poke at it?

And sometimes sellers simply weren't trained to think about what happens after the yes. The sales process ends at the close. Everything after that belongs to customer success, account management, fulfillment, someone else. The seller moves on.

Every one of these patterns costs money, quietly and consistently.

The customer who doesn't hear from you in the days after a purchase is a customer whose brain is busy filling the silence with doubt. This is buyer's remorse, and it forms fastest in the absence of reinforcement. They just committed to something. They're wondering if it was the right call. If you're not there to confirm it was, their own anxiety does the talking.

The customer who hears from you two days after the close, with a warm, no-pressure message that simply asks how the start is going, has an entirely different experience. Their decision gets reinforced. The anxiety doesn't have room to grow. The relationship continues.

One follow-up. Forty-eight hours. That's what the difference costs.

And on the other side of the equation: the customer who's genuinely happy at thirty days is sitting on a goldmine of referrals, reviews, and repeat business that will never get spent if you don't ask. They're not going to volunteer a review. They're not going to walk into their colleague's office and say "you should really call the rep I just worked with." That happens when you create the opening. Most sellers never create the opening because they're already three deals down the pipeline by the time the thirty-day mark arrives.

The after-the-yes system fixes all of this. It's not complicated. It's three touches and two asks, spread across ninety days. The rep who runs it consistently builds a pipeline that generates more leads from existing customers than most people get from all their prospecting combined.

The 48-Hour Touch

Within forty-eight hours of the close, send one short message.

Not a check-in about the transaction. Not a request for something. Not an upsell. A genuinely human, warm, question-led note that says "I'm still here and I'm paying attention."

This is the voice of chapter eleven applied post-close. Short. Personal. Specific to the individual. One question that's easy to answer and shows you're invested in how things are going, not in whether the payment cleared.

"Hey, how's the first day going? Anything surprising?"

That's the whole message. Maybe one additional sentence of context if the situation calls for it. Nothing more. The brevity signals confidence. You're not hovering. You're checking in the way a good colleague would, briefly and genuinely.

The question matters more than the words. "How's the first day going?" is light and curious. "Anything surprising?" opens a door without demanding a walk-through. It invites the customer to share without feeling interrogated. If things are going well, they'll say so, and that brief confirmation deepens the relationship. If something is off, you learn about it now, when it's fixable, instead of in a cancellation email thirty days later.

No upsell. This is important. The 48-hour touch is pure relationship. The moment you attach a product recommendation or a "while I have you" offer to this first post-close message, the customer feels it. The warm check-in becomes a transaction dressed up as care. They can tell the difference, and it poisons the well for every ask that comes later.

Just ask about them. That's the whole job at forty-eight hours.

If the customer responds with something good, great. Reply warmly, celebrate it briefly, and let it breathe. If they respond with a concern, handle it immediately and completely. A customer who raises a concern in the first forty-eight hours and gets a fast, professional response becomes one of your most loyal buyers. They just learned you show up when it matters.

If they don't respond at all, that's fine too. You sent the message. They know you're paying attention. The next touch arrives on day thirty.

The 30-Day Touch

Thirty days in, the customer has had real experience with whatever they bought. The initial energy has settled. They've used it, tested it, integrated it. They have opinions. And those opinions, asked for at the right moment, are worth more than almost anything else in your business.

The thirty-day touch is a results check. One question, and it's the most valuable question you'll ask all year.

"What's better for you since we started?"

This question does something unusual. It assumes the answer is positive. It doesn't ask "how is everything going?" which invites a neutral or vague response. It doesn't ask "any problems?" which invites complaints. It asks what's better, which directs attention toward results and improvement. The framing is optimistic and specific, and it tends to produce responses that match.

When a customer answers "what's better for you since we started?" they're telling you their results in their own words. Those words are worth keeping. They're the raw material for the proof pieces that win your next deal, the kind of social proof covered back in chapter ten. The customer just gave you a testimonial. They just don't know it yet.

This is why the thirty-day touch is described as gold twice over. First, it deepens the relationship by showing you care about outcomes, not just the transaction. Second, it generates the proof that wins the next deal. Both things happen in one question.

Be fully present for their answer. Don't rush to the next agenda item. Let them tell you what changed. Ask a follow-up if they mention something specific. "You mentioned the team is using it more than expected, what's driving that?" The thirty-day touch is a conversation, not a data collection form. Treat it that way.

And then, at the peak of that conversation, when they've just described what's working and why they're glad they made the decision, you make the two asks.

The Two Asks

Most sellers are too shy to make these asks. The ones who aren't shy about it build the best pipelines in the business.

The first ask: the review.

"Would you put what you just told me in a review?"

That's the whole ask. They just said something genuine and specific about what changed for them. You're asking them to say it in a place where other people can read it. The ask is grounded in what they already said, which makes it feel natural rather than grabbed. You're not asking them to come up with something. You're asking them to repeat what they just told you.

Most people, when they're at a genuine high point in a relationship, say yes to this easily. It feels like a small thing. For you, it's anything but small. A specific, authentic review from a real customer is worth dozens of your own marketing messages. It's the borrowed trust from chapter ten applied after the close.

Make the review process easy. Don't just say "could you leave a review somewhere?" Tell them exactly where to go. "We're on Google, if you search us it comes right up." Or "I can send you the direct link." The easier you make the logistics, the more often the review actually gets posted.

The second ask: the referral.

"Who else do you know wrestling with this?"

Not "do you know anyone?" which invites a vague no. Not "if you happen to think of anyone" which signals low expectation and gets it. A specific, direct question that assumes they know someone, which they almost always do.

The phrasing "wrestling with this" matters. It's specific to the problem you solve. It puts the prospect in the frame of their own network and asks them to think about who's dealing with something they recognize. That mental search is productive in a way that "do you know anyone who might need my services?" is not.

Ask this at the thirty-day high point, when the buyer is satisfied and the experience is fresh. Asked when the customer is lukewarm or when the experience is distant, referral asks feel transactional. Asked when the customer is genuinely happy and you've just had a real conversation about their results, the referral ask feels natural. It's a friend telling another friend about something that worked.

If they give you a name, follow up immediately. Within twenty-four hours. A warm referral has a window, and the window closes fast if you let it.

The Flywheel and Repeat and Expand

Here's where this chapter closes the loop with chapter ten.

The proof that wins your next deal comes from the customer you're talking to right now. Their thirty-day results are your next proof touch. Their review is your next borrowed trust. Their referral is your next warm first conversation. The after-the-yes system is the source of the social proof system.

This is the flywheel. Every yes you follow up on produces proof. Proof wins the next deal. The next deal becomes a yes you follow up on. More proof. More deals. The wheel doesn't stop as long as you keep following up on both sides of the close, before and after.

The seller who doesn't follow up after the yes only gets one spin of the wheel per customer. The seller who does gets proof, referrals, and repeat business. That's three spins per customer. The pipelines look completely different over eighteen months. Same number of closes, radically different output.

Now, repeat and expand.

Ninety days in, the customer has lived with the decision long enough to have a real opinion about what's next. The ninety-day touch opens that conversation.

"You've been using this for three months now. Is there anything you wish you'd done bigger from the start?"

That question does two things. It invites honest reflection, which deepens the relationship. And it naturally surfaces appetite for more. A customer who says "honestly, we should have brought in more of the team" is telling you there's a bigger version of what they bought that they're ready to discuss. A customer who says "we're actually thinking about the second location" is handing you the next deal unprompted.

Your existing customers are the warmest pipeline you have. They know you. They trust you. They've had a positive experience. Most sellers work so hard to find new customers that they completely ignore the revenue sitting in the customers they already have.

Every customer gets follow-up. Not just the ones who haven't bought yet. The ones who already have, because those conversations lead to the longest relationships, the best referrals, and the most reliable repeat business.

The fifth conversation happens on both sides of the close. Before the yes, it's the conversation that gets to the deal. After the yes, it's the conversation that funds the next one.

Your Rep

The Drill. Find your most recent closed customer right now. If it's been fewer than forty-eight hours since the close, send the forty-eight-hour touch today. If it's been around thirty days, send the thirty-day touch and make one of the two asks: the review or the referral. Don't wait until the timing is perfect. Send it today.

The Questions.

"How's the first week going? Anything surprising?"

"What's better for you since we started?"

"Would you put what you just told me in a review?"

"Who else do you know wrestling with this?"

Train It. The full after-the-yes sequence, all 90 days of it, is in The Fifth Conversation Workbook at ConvoControl.com/fifthconversation.

Conclusion: One More Conversation

You already know the answer.

You've known it since chapter one, when you looked at the numbers and felt the gap between them in your chest. Many deals take multiple conversations. Many sellers quit early. Everything in between is the fifth conversation, and the fifth conversation belongs to whoever is still willing to have it.

That's the whole book.

One sentence. One gap. One skill that almost nobody trains.

You trained it.

The Whole Book in One Sentence

The deal goes to whoever is willing to have one more conversation.

Read that again, and this time make it personal. Think about the deals you lost last quarter. How many of them actually said no? Or did they go quiet, and then you went quiet, and then weeks passed, and eventually the file sat in your CRM like a gravestone with no date on it?

That's not losing. That's leaving.

You've heard me say it before: most deals aren't lost. They're abandoned. And the rep who abandoned them didn't do it because they were bad at sales. They did it because no one ever trained them on what to do after the room. They got a great first conversation, didn't get the yes, and stood there with nothing in their hands. So they left.

You're not leaving anymore.

This book gave you a system. Not a script, not a set of magic words, not a collection of tricks that make you feel greasy after you use them. A system. A trained skill. The kind of thing that, once it's in your body, you don't have to think about. You just do it, the way a trained athlete doesn't think about footwork in the middle of a match. The footwork is already there.

That's what these seventeen chapters built. And if you ran the drills, if you actually stopped and did the reps instead of just reading about them, you're already different than you were at chapter one. You can feel it.

If you read but didn't rep, that's okay. You know what to do now. The question is when you start.

Here's a plan that makes the answer to that question simple.

The 90-Day Installation Plan

Ninety days is enough time to turn this system into a habit. Habits don't require motivation. They run on their own. That's the whole point.

Here's how to build it.

Weeks 1 and 2: The Audit and the Ladder

Before you add anything new, you need to see what you've got. This is the foundation.

Pull your CRM or your notebook or wherever your deals live. If they live in your head, that's the first problem to fix. Go through every open deal and every dead one you can find. For each deal, count the actual touches it got. Not the touches you planned. The touches it actually received. Find your real quit number.

Most people discover it's lower than they thought. That's not a judgment. That's data. Data you can act on.

While you're in there, sort your deals onto the ladder from chapter 7. Hot deals get touches every 48 to 72 hours. Warm deals get weekly. Stalled deals get every two to three weeks. Long-game deals get quarterly. Put those touches on your calendar right now, not at the end of the week, right now, before you close this book.

Every deal you find that has a stall attached to it gets the follow-up file treatment from chapter 5. Log the trigger, the date, and the re-open question. You don't need to act on all of them today. You just need to have them written down somewhere other than your brain, so the system can carry them instead of you.

By the end of week two, you have a scoreboard of where you actually stand, and every open deal has a next scheduled touch. That's it. That's the whole job for the first two weeks. It's unglamorous and it's powerful.

Weeks 3 Through 6: The Daily Block, the Reopens, and the Value Bank

Now you build the daily practice.

Block the same 60 minutes every single day. Pick a time and defend it. For most people, first thing in the morning before the inbox opens works best. For others, it's end of day before they shut the laptop. Pick the window that's hardest for other people to steal from you, and put follow-up there.

Inside that block, three things happen.

First, you send the touches that are due. You already scheduled them in weeks one and two, so the block isn't about deciding who to touch. It's about doing the touching. That distinction matters more than it sounds. Deciding drains energy. Executing doesn't.

Second, you build your value bank. Give yourself one week to pull together ten market insights, five proof pieces, and a short list of introductions you could make. This is the material from chapter 8. Once it's built, you never stare at a blank screen again. You open the bank, pick something relevant, attach a question, and send it.

Third, you work your reopen questions from chapter 12. Any deal that's been quiet for more than a week gets a depth-appropriate question. Touch two gets a momentum question. Touch five gets a status question. Touch nine gets an honesty question. You don't have to figure this out in the moment because you already have the questions. You just match the depth to the deal and send it.

By the end of week six, the daily block is a habit. It doesn't feel like a chore anymore. It feels like training, because it is training. The pipeline starts to look different. Deals that were quiet are responding. Deals you wrote off are coming back. And you're building a reputation, one touch at a time, as the rep who stays in the conversation when everyone else leaves.

Weeks 7 Through 12: The Long Game, the Scoreboard, and After the Yes

This is where the system compounds.

Every deal that doesn't belong on the hot, warm, or stalled rung moves to the long-game list. These are your "next year" and "check back in Q2" deals. Log them with a trigger, a date, and a quarterly touch scheduled. Put an alert on the deals where a trigger event would change the conversation, a new funding round, a new fiscal year, a new person in the chair. When the event fires, you have a reason to reach out that has nothing to do with your quota.

Start keeping the four numbers from chapter 16 every Friday. Five minutes. Touches per closed deal. Reply rate by touch type. Deals revived. Deals lost to silence on your side. After a month of tracking, the data tells you things no coach could. It shows you your real quit point, your best channel, your best send window, and which questions get answered. You stop guessing and start adjusting.

And every time you close a deal, do the after-the-yes sequence from chapter 17. The 48-hour touch. The 30-day check-in. The review ask and the referral ask. Every yes you follow up on creates the proof that wins the next deal. The flywheel spins, and the longer it spins, the less you have to push it.

By week twelve, the fifth conversation is just what you do. Other reps are still quitting at touch two. You're still in the room, months later, on conversations your competitors don't know are happening.

That's the plan. It's not complicated. It just requires you to actually do it.

The Graveyard Challenge

Here's your first assignment from outside the chapters. Not a rep, not a drill. A challenge.

This month, go back to your graveyard. Find ten deals that got one conversation and silence. Ten deals you walked away from, not because the prospect said no, but because you stopped asking. They might be in your CRM under a label like "closed lost" or "no response" or just sitting in an old spreadsheet you stopped looking at six months ago.

Find ten. Pull them out.

Now run the playbook on each one.

First, check whether it's actually dead or just sleeping. Has enough time passed that something in their world might have changed? A new quarter, a new role, a new budget, a new problem? If yes, you've got a reason to reach back out that isn't "I noticed I never followed up, sorry about that."

Second, pick the right question. Not "just checking in." A real question that quotes their situation, their language, the specific thing they told you they were worried about. That question is the master key from chapter 12. Use it.

Third, send it and log the result. Don't batch-blast all ten at once. Space them over the month. One or two a week. That way, if some of them respond, you can actually handle the conversations without getting buried.

Picture a rep, call her Dana. She's been in software sales for three years and she has a list of what she calls her "zombie deals," the ones she gave one shot and then never touched again. She pulls twelve of them out one Monday morning and sends honest, specific reopen questions to each one over the course of a month. Three of them respond. One of those three becomes a real conversation. One of those real conversations closes.

That deal was already in her pipeline. She just stopped visiting it.

Your graveyard holds deals you've already paid for with your time and your prospecting work. The cost of reaching back out is a few minutes and a good question. The upside is a deal that was already warmed up by a conversation someone else paid for, that someone being the version of you who ran that first call.

Pull ten. Run the playbook. See what comes back.

You don't have to rescue all ten. You just have to remember that some of them aren't dead. They're waiting.

The Graduation Question

You've read the book. You know the framework. You have the questions, the ladder, the value bank, the scoreboard, the reopen sequences, and the after-the-yes flywheel.

Reading built the knowledge.

Now comes the part most people skip. Most people read. Few people rep.

The reps are where this actually transfers. Every drill block in this book pointed you toward a real action on a real deal in your real pipeline. If you ran those drills, you've already got reps under your belt. The knowledge is starting to sit in your body instead of just your head. That's a different thing. That's how gymnasts train before competition. Not by reading about the routine. By running the routine until the body knows it without permission from the brain.

The ConvoDojo exists for exactly that reason. It's the live weekly practice arena where you train conversations under pressure, not in theory. You get feedback in real time. You get repetition with resistance. You get the kind of training that turns a concept you understand into a skill you can execute when the moment matters.

The workbook takes the drills from every chapter and stretches them into a full 90-day practice sequence. It's structured the same way this book is, three parts, progressive, each week building on the last. If you want the habit to stick, the workbook is how you lock it in.

And then there's the question I want to ask you the way this book has taught you to ask questions.

Want this trained into you until you can't get it wrong?

That's what the Black Belt mastery program is for. One-on-one, personalized, built around your pipeline and your deals and your specific stuck points. The application is at ConvoControl.com/fifthconversation.

Everything you need to go further lives there. The workbook. The ConvoDojo. The Blueprint course. The mastery program. All of it at ConvoControl.com/fifthconversation.

One more conversation is all it takes. With a stalled deal, with an old ghost, with a prospect who's been warming in your long-game list for six months. One more conversation, the one your competition never made it to.

Go have it.

So, How Can We Help You?

Here's the full ConvoControl ladder. Start wherever you are. Go as far as you want to go.

The ConvoControl Series

Seven books, one system. Questions Close Deals built the foundation. Everything Is Sales expanded the frame. Win at Work brought it inside organizations. The Answer Is No...For Now handled resistance in the room. Exit Strategy covered the hardest conversations. Parenting a Parent applied the system to the most personal conversations of all. And this book, The Fifth Conversation, picked up where all of them left off: the moment after the first call ends, when the real work begins.

All available at ConvoControl.com/fifthconversation.

The Fifth Conversation Workbook

The 90-day follow-up practice system. Every drill from this book extended into a daily and weekly sequence. Scorecards, reopen-question banks, ladder templates, and the full after-the-yes sequence. If the book is the map, the workbook is the training log. ConvoControl.com/fifthconversation.

ConvoDojo

The live weekly practice arena. Real conversations, real pressure, real-time feedback. This is where the reps happen. Not in theory. In the dojo. ConvoControl.com/fifthconversation.

The Conversation Control Blueprint Course

A complete self-paced program covering the full ConvoControl system, from mental positioning and question strategy through follow-up, cadence, and close. For reps and founders who want to build the entire skill set, not just one piece of it. ConvoControl.com/fifthconversation.

Black Belt Mastery Coaching

One-on-one with Tara. Application only. For the rep or founder who is done learning and ready to drill, with personalized feedback on their real deals, their real pipeline, and their specific gaps. No price listed here. If you want it, apply at ConvoControl.com/fifthconversation and we'll take it from there.

Corporate Training and Keynotes

Tara works with sales teams and organizations that want the ConvoControl system built into their culture, not just handed to them as a book. Live training, on-site or virtual, built around your team's actual pipeline and challenges. Keynotes available for conferences, sales kickoffs, and leadership events. Reach out at ConvoControl.com/fifthconversation.

About the Author

Tara Shuler is the founder of ConvoControl and creator of the ConvoDojo, and she's spent more than 25 years doing the thing this book is actually about: staying in the conversation when it would be easier to walk away.

She's personally closed over $50 million across B2B, B2C, and live events, not by being the loudest voice in the room, but by asking better questions and following up when everyone else disappeared.

Before sales, she was a Level 9 competitive gymnast and a gymnastics coach. That background is where the philosophy comes from. Gymnastics taught her that performance is trained, not hoped for. You don't rise to the occasion. You fall back on how you've trained. She brought that mindset to every sales floor she's worked on and to every rep she's coached since.

She built ConvoControl because she kept watching talented people learn the right concepts and then fail to execute them under pressure. The concepts weren't the problem. The practice was. ConvoDojo exists to fix that.

Tara lives in St. Petersburg, Florida.

ConvoControl.com

www.ingramcontent.com/pod-product-compliance
Lightning Source LLC
LaVergne TN
LVHW100142061126
851857LV00010B/195
* 9 7 9 8 9 9 6 9 5 3 0 7 3 *